I0149967

Known
and
Loved

COLLEGE
PRESS
www.collegepress.com

KNOWN AND LOVED: Women's Prayer Journey through 1 John
© 2023 by College Press Publishing. All rights reserved.

Published by College Press Publishing
Joplin, Missouri
www.collegepress.com

ISBN: 978-0-89900-902-5 (spiral bound)
ISBN: 978-0-89900-900-1 (paperback)

All Scripture quotations, unless otherwise indicated, are taken from the Holy Bible, New International Version®, NIV®. Copyright ©1973, 1978, 1984, 2011 by Biblica, Inc.® Used by permission of Zondervan. All rights reserved worldwide. www.zondervan.com The "NIV" and "New International Version" are trademarks registered in the United States Patent and Trademark Office by Biblica, Inc.®

Cover Graphics and Design by **Christina Schofield**

RECOMMENDATIONS

In my work with women in all seasons of life living in every corner of the planet, I have come to understand that there is a desire shared by all of us. Whether we are looking down at grooves worn in the path we have walked with the Lord over decades of relationship, or we are just taking our first tentative laps together, we all long to look up to the One we are walking with and feel seen, valuable, and precious. In the pages of this book, Jessica invites us to open communication with the Father in a way that is not intimidating and not overwhelming. She invites us into rhythms that have the potential to transform our hearts and lives. She invites us to come to the unavoidable conclusion through time spent in his presence that we are his. We are worthy. We are known and loved.

Denise Beck
Executive Director of Velvet Ashes

If you have been looking for guidance in revitalizing your prayer life, you've found it! In the same way that the letter of 1 John is clear and uncomplicated (light vs. dark, truth vs. deceit, right vs. wrong), so too is Jessica's approach to study, prayer, and meditation. The variety of prayer practices included, combined with the voices of other trustworthy women, keep this guide fresh and motivational. And the concise study expectations for each day also make it doable! From the boardroom to the laundry room, every woman, in every season, needs to sit in the presence of the Lord. *Known and Loved* is the key that will usher you right through that door.

Beth DeFazio
Professor of Biblical Communication
Ozark Christian College

In a world that is seemingly always-changing, never-stopping, and full of chaos, this book is a welcomed breath of fresh air. Jessica invites us to bring our whole selves into a sacred space with the Father -- submitting our minds, hearts, and even physical bodies to His presence. We are not simply asked to read about His love, but to fully experience and embrace it. Through her words, I am reminded that I am not simply allowed to be in a relationship with the Creator of the universe, but I am pursued by, united with, and delighted in by Him.

Maggie Schade
Community Impact Minister
Christ's Church of Oronogo

TABLE OF CONTENTS

ABOUT THE CONTRIBUTORS

Allow me to introduce you to some of my nearest and dearest:

Rhonda Hayward – After 30+ years of Bible translation work in Papua New Guinea, Rhonda became an OCC Residence Director (a.k.a., my dorm mom). She is both the gentlest of listeners and the fiercest of prayer warriors – a woman I can always trust to help me truly stop and listen to the Holy Spirit.

Danielle Wheeler – Since her family's transition from China to the U.S. several years ago, Danielle has shaped my prayer life in significant ways. She is the founder of "Velvet Ashes" – a ministry for women serving cross-culturally – and is now also a licensed Spiritual Director where she continues to help others listen for the voice of God.

Michelle Schaffer – For the past several years, Michelle has been a steady voice of wisdom, encouragement, and perspective. She is a gifted worship leader, a humble and attentive listener, a godly wife and an incredible mom; in recent months she has been helping equip families through a government agency in Indiana.

Caitlyn Edwards – My college roommate, ministry partner, and dear friend. Caitlyn consistently models Jesus' love, pursues Jesus intentionally through every season, and continuously strives for others to know Him. She currently lives in Japan, serving as a church planter with Mustard Seed Network.

Alexandria Brazle – When imagining how I wanted this book to "feel" when people read it, I imagined Alex's living room: a place where people feel truly seen and treasured for who they are, where both their gut-wrenching questions and raw, messy answers are welcome. Alex is a close friend, an author, wife, and mom of two beautiful girls.

Kim McIntire – Several years ago, Kim and I met while serving at a local ministry for at-risk kids. Her heart for people and passion for the Lord was evident from day one, and since then she has continued to be a mentor and fervent prayer warrior in my life. This fall, she also just released her new book, "Abiding Conversations"!

SPECIAL THANKS TO:

Christina Schofield,
Melinda Vaughn,
and Aurora Rayos

*Thank you for the ways that you shaped
and impacted this book.
Your prayers, encouragement, and input
throughout this process have been invaluable!*

FOREWORD

I like young people. I like their vitality, their passion when they latch on to a purpose, their spontaneity, their ability to jump into a challenge without being too put off by fear of failure. At the same time, young people can often charge headlong into the great unknown without a thought or a plan. Weighing the cost might be considered a vast waste of time when there is so much at stake!

And that is why I like old people. Old people may lack the sparkle of youth, but for those who have walked with Jesus year after year, well, they have something that young people long for – wisdom.

Jessica Skiles is an old soul in a young body. I have had the honor of being in a mentor relationship (not sure who was mentoring who!) when Jessica was a student at Ozark Christian College just a few years ago. She was delightful from day one. Don't get me wrong – she dealt with the normal concerns of a college student – *"Will I ever find the right mate?" "Should I do this internship?" "How do I deal with this difficult person in the dorm?" "How do I stay motivated in my classes when the workload is so heavy?"*

But even then, the wisdom of God was growing in her because . . . She. Desired. Him. God matures the believer who seeks him and it is evident in the wisdom they carry. That is why it is so easy to recommend this book: I trust Jessica's words because I trust Jessica's wisdom. So enjoy going deeper in your walk with our Lord as you use this guide through I John. I assure you it comes from the heart of a faithful young lady who is wise beyond her years.

And by the way – she graduated from college with honors, impacted our school with her character and maturity, and got the young man for whom she had prayed. They are now awaiting the birth of their first child!

JULIE GARISS

Co-director of Life and Ministry Preparation Center

Ozark Christian College

INTRODUCTION

"This is love: not that we loved God,
but that he loved us."
– 1 John 4:10[1]

Too often, I have thought of prayer as an obligation – a way to prove to God that I love him. But here, Jesus totally flips that paradigm. He changes it from "my love, my ability, my goodness," to "his love, his ability, his goodness." *I* am *first* known and loved by God: that alone is the reason I can approach God's throne with my sins, praises, and requests.

To be known and loved by God: that is the invitation of this book, the invitation of 1 John, the invitation of Jesus Christ. Our prayer is that these pages become a sacred space for you: a place where, when you don't know how to begin the conversation, the table is set for you to meet with the Holy Spirit.

What does that look like practically? This five-week journey is a compilation of guided prayer practices through 1 John. These are written by myself and a handful of my most trusted friends and mentors – women who have each uniquely shaped my prayer journey and often been a mouthpiece of the Holy Spirit in my life. We will practice seven different forms of prayer, engaging each chapter in a variety of ways – gratitude, obedience, study, and art to name a few. Some may feel awkward at first, and others may really "click" for you in a way you never experienced before. Either way, we pray this provides a unique opportunity for you to experience God with every part of who you are – mind, body and spirit – and develop a rhythm to commune with God through his Word.

SNAPSHOT OF 1 JOHN

Author: Who wrote this?

This book is often credited to John the Apostle[2]: a Jewish fisherman who became a close friend and follower of Jesus.[3] In his writing, he often referred to himself as "the disciple whom Jesus loved." He was articulate, poetic, and perceptive – nicknamed by Jesus a "son of thunder" (Mk. 3:17), though his passion sometimes misfired (Luke 9:49-56). However, as he walked with Jesus and was transformed by the Holy Spirit, a fierce love for Christ, the church, and the lost swelled within him.[4] Eventually, he became a prominent leader in the Jerusalem church and a bishop in the church of Ephesus.[5]

Audience: Who is this written to?

John likely wrote this letter to his church in Ephesus (or a nearby church in Asia Minor) towards the end of the first century.[6] Historically, this was a turbulent time: tyrannical emperors, pressure from the imperial cult, and varying levels of Christian persecution characterized life in the Roman Empire.[7] In addition to external pressures, within the church a group of "intellectuals" had emerged. Their teachings dismissed both the gravity of their own sin and the saving power of the cross.[8] Eventually, these false teachers split off, leaving the remaining congregation to wrestle with the genuineness of their own faith.

Purpose: Why did he write it?

John's letter invited these remaining believers to draw close to God and one another. He affirmed that their faith was grounded in the truth, and because they believed *in* him their acceptance *by* him was also assured (1 John 1:3, 5:13).[9] He wanted them to remain true to what they had been taught (1 John 2:20-27) and have confidence in God's gift of salvation.

WEEK 1

1 John 1:1-10

[1] That which was from the beginning, which we have heard, which we have seen with our eyes, which we have looked at and our hands have touched—this we proclaim concerning the Word of life. [2] The life appeared; we have seen it and testify to it, and we proclaim to you the eternal life, which was with the Father and has appeared to us. [3] We proclaim to you what we have seen and heard, so that you also may have fellowship with us. And our fellowship is with the Father and with his Son, Jesus Christ. [4] We write this to make our joy complete.

[5] This is the message we have heard from him and declare to you: God is light; in him there is no darkness at all. [6] If we claim to have fellowship with him and yet walk in the darkness, we lie and do not live out the truth. [7] But if we walk in the light, as he is in the light, we have fellowship with one another, and the blood of Jesus, his Son, purifies us from all sin.

[8] If we claim to be without sin, we deceive ourselves and the truth is not in us. [9] If we confess our sins, he is faithful and just and will forgive us our sins and purify us from all unrighteousness. [10] If we claim we have not sinned, we make him out to be a liar and his word is not in us.

Palms Up, Palms Down
– Jessica Skiles –

Pause:

Dear friend, there is one who has loved you perfectly. *Perfectly.* He has experienced first-hand every harsh word you have spoken, every ugly attitude and bad hair day – and has continued to pursue you. Your Creator God has invited you to come in *close*: to be seen, to be cleansed, to be loved.

In the busyness of life, this truth often just hits the surface and rolls right off – it's hard to be still and allow it to sink in. So before we go any further, would you be willing to stop for just a moment? Set a timer on your phone for one minute, then set it face down beside you. Close your eyes, breathe in big, deep breaths, and ask God to allow this truth to settle deep into your heart and illuminate your next few weeks in 1 John.

Opening Prayer:

Jesus, thank you for drawing close to us. Would you soften my heart and open my ears to hear what you have to say?

Prayer Practice:[10]

Read through 1 John 1, mentally highlighting things that God is calling us to *release* and things he is inviting us to *receive*. As you sit, squarely plant your feet and hold your hands out in front of you in a posture of surrender. With eyes closed, turn your palms towards the ground and begin to *release* these things in prayer: tell God about that sin struggle, the crippling doubt, or the worries that keep pulling your attention from him.

When you feel the weight has dropped from your hands, flip your palms upwards into a position of *receiving*. Thank God for the goodness he has revealed to you in this passage – his invitation of relationship, his promise to forgive, etc. Ask for his help in receiving these things.

Feel free to switch back and forth between these positions as many times as needed.

Closing Prayer:

Jesus, thank you for coming close to us. Thank you for pulling us from death into life; sin into forgiveness; darkness into light. Thank you that we don't have to hide from you, but instead you invite us to show you our sin and our doubt, and you transform it. Please give us the ability to trust you fully – to draw in closer, to confess our sins openly, and to walk in your light. Amen.

What are you calling me to release?

_____

_____

_____

_____

_____

_____

_____

_____

_____

_____

_____

_____

_____

What are you inviting me to receive?

_____

_____

_____

_____

_____

_____

_____

_____

_____

_____

_____

_____

_____

Know, Obey, Confess, Give Thanks
– Jessica Skiles –

Pause:

Breathe in. Breathe out. Breathe in. Breathe out.

So often, we take for granted the very things that keep us alive. We go about our day without even a passing thought to the heart pumping blood through our veins, the lungs taking in each breath, the sun maintaining light and life on the earth. How much more do we forget the Spirit of God sustaining all of those things – our heart, our lungs, our world?

At this time, I want to invite you to remember. Set a timer for one minute and breathe slow, big breaths. Use this time to visualize the ways you have seen God's provision in your life: through prayer, his people, his Word, and creation.

Opening Prayer:

Jesus, please open up my ears to hear your voice, my heart to understand, and my hands to obey what you speak in this passage. May you be glorified in my thoughts, my words, my attitudes, and my actions.

Prayer Practice:

Read through 1 John 1 slowly, asking God these questions as you go:

1. What truth do you want me to know?
2. What command do I need to obey?
3. What sin do I need to confess?
4. What gift or promise can I thank you for?

For some, it may be helpful to jot down a bullet list under each category while reading, then praying over that list at the end. For others, immediately praying what you see as you read may feel more natural ("Lord, please grow this characteristic in me," "please help me to release this thing," etc.). Feel free to do whatever works best for you!

Closing Prayer:

Jesus, thank you for being a good and gentle Savior. You invite me to walk with you, and in your brilliance, I am clearly seen. Your light washes every sin and blemish it touches. In Christ, I am cleansed, I am washed, I am forgiven. Thank you for your grace. Give me strength to continue in your light today. Amen.

What truth do you want me to know?

_____

_____

_____

_____

_____

_____

_____

_____

_____

_____

_____

_____

What command do I need to obey?

_____

_____

_____

_____

_____

_____

_____

_____

_____

_____

_____

_____

What sin do I need to confess?

_____

_____

_____

_____

_____

_____

_____

_____

_____

_____

_____

_____

What gift or promise can I thank you for?

_____

_____

_____

_____

_____

_____

_____

_____

_____

_____

_____

_____

Study
– Jessica Skiles –

Pause:

Light. Life. Fellowship.[11]

These concepts are the lifeblood of 1 John: they thread together every truth, promise and command, because they are God's invitation to *be with him.* They are pictures of his character that we get to share in.

For the next minute (feel free to set a timer), I'd like you to visualize God inviting you into these things. Ask him for strength to step into the light and life he has offered. Ask him for a soft heart that desires to draw closer to him.

Opening Prayer:

Jesus, thank you for being light and life; for inviting me to walk with you. Please calm my anxious thoughts so that I can truly listen to your voice. I give you my mind, my heart, and my strength. Please help me to hear and obey what you have to show me today.

Study:

In the beginning . . . God (Genesis 1:1-5).

God spoke, and light sprung out of a void of darkness – setting time, contrast, and the creation story into motion. The story to begin all stories, spun by the Word of God.

In the beginning . . . God (John 1:1-5, 9-14).

The Word of God stepped into our existence, and light pierced the darkness. The Creator – the Light of the world – set his story in the lives of ordinary people and drew them into the family of God.

From the beginning . . . God (1 John 1:1-7).

The Word of God appeared, and light united with the human heart. He pulled us into h*is* story, *his* community by the cross, and backed it with every fulfilled prophecy, miraculous provision, healing touch and resurrected encounter.

This story is one that God has been writing since before time and space began! In a nutshell, John is starting out this letter by saying, "God himself has come near to us. We have seen him, we know this is true! The fullest life and the richest joy you can imagine is within your reach: I want to tell you about it!"

Over the next few minutes, open your Bible and examine these three passages. Take note of the details, highlight repeated words and themes, and ask God to draw your attention to what he wants you to see.

Closing Prayer:

Father, your story of grace has extended from cover to cover. From Adam all through Israel, the Apostles, and the Church, you have heaped grace on undeserving people. When we handed you sin, you handed us friendship. You spoke, and light drove out the darkness. Where death had taken hold, you breathed life. Thank you for your kindness to us. Please give us eyes to see you and hearts that receive you; we are yours. Amen.

God, what do you want me to see?

Truth, Lies, and Declaration
– Jessica Skiles –

Pause:

I began mulling over this passage while sitting on my back patio – crickets chirping, cherry pop setting by my lawn chair, and far too many mosquitoes swarming around my head. It had been several days since I had a really focused time of study and prayer, and it was taking me a while to settle in. "Jesus," I asked, "will you point out to me the truths here that I'm not truly believing?" Sometimes, I find it helpful to imagine that Jesus is sitting next to me while I'm praying – maybe he's listening while sipping a cup of coffee, offering advice, or pointing out a line in my Bible he wants me to notice.[1] As you settle into your own space – maybe it's your living room, front porch, a coffee shop – take a minute (set a timer) to imagine that Jesus is sitting there with you. Ask him to open your eyes to his truth.

Opening Prayer:

Jesus, will you point out to me the truth you want me to see? Would you uproot the lies I've held onto and replace them with your Word?

Truth, Lies, And Declaration:

What we *believe* determines how we *behave*. If I believe a chair is sturdy, I won't think twice about sitting in it. If I believe my doctor is qualified, I'll follow her prescription. If I believe God is good, I will be more likely to obey him. The question is, are the things we believe about

---

1. If this feels uncomfortable for you, lean into the fact that this is *what Jesus did* with his disciples during his time on earth. He swapped stories, gave advice, had cookouts, sat side by side with friends and talked about real everyday problems. This is a way that God has graciously invited his people to know him!

God *true?* Unless we continue to hold up our beliefs against Scripture, it is easy for lies to creep in and twist our understanding of who God is.

Over the next several minutes, read through 1 John 1 a couple of times and ask God to guide you through these steps.

- **Truth**: Ask God *"what truth do you want me to see in this chapter?"* As you read, write down the truths that stand out to you.

- **Lies:** Ask *"Are there any lies that I have been believing that oppose this truth?"* Renounce these and replace them with the truth that God just showed you.

- **Declaration:** Write down a declaration and read it often! Place it somewhere visible – on your mirror, phone lock screen, etc. – and let this truth take root in your heart throughout this week.

Here's an example!

Truth: If I confess my sin, God is faithful to forgive.

Lie: I can't be honest with God; I'm too dirty to be accepted as I truly am.

Declaration: God makes good on his promise to forgive! I can come out of hiding, because in Christ's light I find healing, joy, community and hope. I am forgiven!

Closing Prayer:

Jesus, thank you for showing yourself to me. I believe that these things are true . . . help me to live by them. Amen.

What truth do you want me to see in this chapter?

_____

_____

_____

_____

_____

_____

_____

_____

_____

_____

_____

_____

_____

Are there any lies that I have been believing that oppose this truth?

_____

_____

_____

_____

_____

_____

_____

_____

_____

_____

_____

_____

What declaration of truth do you have for me today?

_____

_____

_____

_____

_____

_____

_____

_____

_____

_____

_____

_____

_____

Lectio Divina
– Jessica Skiles –

Pause:

"God is light, in him there is no darkness at all."
– 1 John 1:5

Sometimes, the darkness can be suffocating – leaving us feeling lost, alone, and afraid. When our greatest fears are pressing in, God has offered this promise to be *light*: offering hope, giving direction, kicking out fear, and producing life. He is pure and total light.

For the next minute, allow yourself to soak in this verse. Take a long, deep breath in and (as you inhale) think on the phrase, *"God is light."* Then, as you let out that breath, exhale the rest of the verse, *"in him there is no darkness at all."* Continue to repeat this process for the next minute.

Opening Prayer:

Jesus, thank you for bringing light into my darkness – you have given me hope, you have lit a path for me to walk on, you have cast out my fear, you have brought me to life. Please open my eyes to see and my heart to obey what you have for me today. I am yours.

Lectio Divina:

Today's invitation involves a very old prayer practice, one that Christians have used to engage with Scripture for the past 1500 years! *Lectio Divina* has an intentional "looseness" to it, built on the understanding that God's Word is living and active.[12] It focuses on genuinely opening ourselves to God, because we are invited to a very real encounter with our Heavenly Father! As you dive in, allow yourself the next 10-15 minutes and ask God to guide you through these four steps.

1. Read 1 John 1:5-10 once slowly. Ask God to draw your attention to a *word* or a *phrase*, and then write it down.

2. Read the same passage a second time. What *image* comes to mind? Take time to either draw or describe what you see.

3. Read it through a third time. What *meaning* is God highlighting for you in this phrase or passage? Allow yourself to respond to God during this step – whether through words, song, or something else that he may have prompted during this time.

4. Finally, read through this one more time, slowly. Simply rest in his presence and allow this text to wash over you as you prepare to move forward into your day.

Closing Prayer:

Jesus, I know that I am a sinner. So often, I plug my ears and close my eyes to my sin . . . but you see me. You know everything that I have done and should've done. Would you take these habits that are not honoring to you and trade them for the fruit of your Spirit? I need you, Jesus. Thank you for drawing me into your light and forgiveness. Amen.

Word or Phrase

Image

How are you inviting me to respond?

_____

_____

_____

_____

_____

_____

_____

_____

_____

_____

_____

_____

_____

_____

_____

_____

_____

_____

_____

_____

_____

_____

_____

_____

_____

_____

_____

_____

Obedience
– Danielle Wheeler –

Pause:

Enter into silence. Closing your eyes, breathe deeply to help quiet your mind. Allow distracting thoughts to drift away as you become aware of God's presence with you. Inhale and exhale. God is here with you. Sit in the silence with the Lord for as long as you'd like.

Opening Prayer:

Father, Son, and Holy Spirit, I acknowledge your presence here with me now. I remember that I am surrounded and enfolded by your love for me. May your Spirit lead me into what you have for me today.

Obedience:

Slowly read through the following verse, inviting God to speak to you.

> *"But if we confess our sins, he is faithful and just and will*
> *forgive us our sins and purify us from all unrighteousness."*
> *– 1 John 1:9*

Prayerfully examine your heart and ask the Lord, *"Is there an area of sin in my life that you would like to shine light upon today?"*

You might ask yourself, *"When in my life do I feel far from you, God?"*

Pause and wait. See if God brings something to mind.

If something comes to mind, allow it to come. Feelings of shame or guilt or frustration will want to shove these thoughts away. Invite them in. Hold this area of your life before the presence of God who sees and knows all of you.

Invite God to show you his posture towards you in this moment. What do his eyes look like? What does he do with his arms? His hands?

Receive his love for you.

Acknowledge to God how you have not lived in his desire for you in this area of your life.

Receive his forgiveness. Allow his cleansing to wash over you.

Rest in his love.

Closing Prayer:

You might use the words of Psalm 51 to close in prayer.

Have mercy on me, O God,
according to Your loving devotion;
according to Your great compassion,
blot out my transgressions.
Wash me clean of my iniquity
and cleanse me from my sin.
For I know my transgressions,
and my sin is always before me.
Against You, You only, have I sinned
and done what is evil in Your sight,
so that You may be proved right when You speak
and blameless when You judge.
Surely I was brought forth in iniquity;
I was sinful when my mother conceived me.

Surely You desire truth in the inmost being;
*   You teach me wisdom in the inmost place.*
Purify me with hyssop, and I will be clean;
*   wash me, and I will be whiter than snow.*
Let me hear joy and gladness;
*   let the bones You have crushed rejoice.*
Hide Your face from my sins
*   and blot out all my iniquities.*
Create in me a clean heart, O God,
*   and renew a right spirit within me.*
Cast me not away from Your presence;
*   take not Your Holy Spirit from me.*
Restore to me the joy of Your salvation,
*   and sustain me with a willing spirit.*

Amen.

Is there an area of sin in my life that you would like to shine light upon today?

_____

_____

_____

_____

_____

_____

_____

When in my life do I feel far from you, God?

_____

_____

_____

_____

_____

_____

_____

What do you have to say to me today? What is your posture towards me?

_____

_____

_____

_____

_____

_____

_____

_____

Art

– Jessica Skiles –

Pause:

To be truly seen for who we are – and to still be loved, trusted, and brought near – this is one of the greatest gifts we can ever receive. The presence of a close friend: a place where secrets are no longer tucked away, but shared; where comparison and performance fade away. This is the kind of family God's people are invited into, and John is bursting with delight as he extends the invitation: "we write this to make our joy complete" (1 John 1:4).

Take a moment to sit with God – the Father who loves you in this way. He *sees* you, and he pulls you close; you are cleansed and accepted in his presence. Set a timer for one minute and allow this truth to wash over you.

Opening Prayer:

Jesus, thank you for drawing me close. Give me the strength and the wisdom to know that love. Help me not to run away.

Prayer Practice:

God often uses art to carry truth down the long journey from *head* to *heart*. Stories, poems, melodies, paintings – they slide past our defenses and take root in a very personal way.

A Father's Invitation

Come in close to me
My promise, you can trust
I will not let you crumble
So lean upon my love
Don't fear the light, oh daughter
But show your heart to me
Let true love wash away your shame
I long to make you clean
Oh child, I have loved you
So lean into my grace
Here at my side, you're purified
So come and live with me

41

Read through 1 John 1. With this text in mind, read the poem below and ask God, *"what do you want me to see?"* Spend some time reflecting with him on the following questions:

- What truth about God does this point me to?

- What truth about my identity in Christ does this remind me of?

- What truth about the Church does this help me understand?

As various thoughts and emotions rise to the surface, lift each up in prayer. Maybe you feel overwhelmed by the grace he has extended; thank him for his kindness to you! Does God feel distant? Share your struggle with him. Allow those emotions – good and bad – to become a connecting place for you and God as you extend each one back to him.

Closing Prayer:

Jesus, thank you for meeting me here – for pulling me close, for washing me clean. Help me to lean into your presence today. Amen.

What truth about God does this point me to?

_____

_____

_____

_____

_____

_____

_____

_____

What truth about my identity in Christ does this remind me of?

_____

_____

_____

_____

_____

_____

_____

_____

What truth about the Church does this help me understand?

_____

_____

_____

_____

_____

_____

_____

_____

WEEK 2

1 John 2:1-29

¹My dear children, I write this to you so that you will not sin. But if anybody does sin, we have an advocate with the Father – Jesus Christ, the Righteous One. ²He is the atoning sacrifice for our sins, and not only for ours but also for the sins of the whole world.

³We know that we have come to know him if we keep his commands. ⁴Whoever says, "I know him," but does not do what he commands is a liar, and the truth is not in that person. ⁵But if anyone obeys his word, love for God is truly made complete in them. This is how we know we are in him: ⁶Whoever claims to live in him must live as Jesus did.

⁷Dear friends, I am not writing you a new command but an old one, which you have had since the beginning. This old command is the message you have heard. ⁸Yet I am writing you a new command; its truth is seen in him and in you, because the darkness is passing and the true light is already shining.

⁹Anyone who claims to be in the light but hates a brother or sister is still in the darkness. ¹⁰Anyone who loves their brother and sister lives in the light, and there is nothing in them to make them stumble. ¹¹But anyone who hates a brother or sister is in the darkness and walks around in the darkness. They do not know where they are going, because the darkness has blinded them.

¹²I am writing to you, dear children,
> because your sins have been forgiven on account of his name.
¹³I am writing to you, fathers,
> because you know him who is from the beginning.
I am writing to you, young men,
> because you have overcome the evil one.

[14] I write to you, dear children,
> because you know the Father.

I write to you, fathers,
> because you know him who is from the beginning.

I write to you, young men,
> because you are strong,
> and the word of God lives in you,
> and you have overcome the evil one.

[15] Do not love the world or anything in the world. If anyone loves the world, love for the Father[d] is not in them. [16] For everything in the world – the lust of the flesh, the lust of the eyes, and the pride of life – comes not from the Father but from the world. [17] The world and its desires pass away, but whoever does the will of God lives forever.

[18] Dear children, this is the last hour; and as you have heard that the antichrist is coming, even now many antichrists have come. This is how we know it is the last hour. [19] They went out from us, but they did not really belong to us. For if they had belonged to us, they would have remained with us; but their going showed that none of them belonged to us.

[20] But you have an anointing from the Holy One, and all of you know the truth.[e] [21] I do not write to you because you do not know the truth, but because you do know it and because no lie comes from the truth. [22] Who is the liar? It is whoever denies that Jesus is the Christ. Such a person is the antichrist – denying the Father and the Son. [23] No one who denies the Son has the Father; whoever acknowledges the Son has the Father also.

[24] As for you, see that what you have heard from the beginning remains in you. If it does, you also will remain in the Son and in the Father. [25] And this is what he promised us – eternal life.

[26] I am writing these things to you about those who are trying to lead you astray. [27] As for you, the anointing you received from him remains in you, and you do not need anyone to teach you. But as his anointing teaches you about all things and as that anointing is real, not counterfeit – just as it has taught you, remain in him.

[28] And now, dear children, continue in him, so that when he appears we may be confident and unashamed before him at his coming.

[29] If you know that he is righteous, you know that everyone who does what is right has been born of him.

Palms Up, Palms Down
– Jessica Skiles –

Pause:

1 John 2:1 tells us that Jesus is our advocate: a legal term representing a helper in distress, advisor for the next step, and legal defender. As we each stand in the courtroom of God, with no defense against the devil's accusations, Jesus Christ, our Advocate, steps in. He is the strong, gentle hand on our shoulder, the guiding voice in our ear. He approaches the Judge's bench and confidently declares our innocence: "Her debt is paid in full." Why is he so confident? Because he paid every last drop that our sin required, and he allows his righteousness – his sacrifice – to speak in our defense.

Set a time for the next minute, breathe deeply, then close your eyes to visualize this scene. How does Jesus react to accusations presented against you? What emotions rise within you as Jesus approaches the bench – paying your penalty and pleading your case? How does God react to Jesus' request?

Opening Prayer:

Jesus, thank you for being my advocate – for speaking in my defense, for giving me strength and wisdom when I have none. Would you open my heart and mind to hear you speak?

Prayer Practice:

For today's practice, I would like to invite you to kneel. Read through 1 John 2:1-2 slowly, holding your hands out in front of you in surrender. Throughout the next several minutes, ask God these two questions:

1. *"What sins and situations do I need to release to you today?"* Turn your palms downward as you express your worries, frustrations, and sin habits. He invites us to give these to him!

2. *"What are you inviting me to receive in exchange?"* God offers to transform our ashes into beauty, guilt into forgiveness, worries into provision. As you release your burdens to him, would you ask him to replace them with good things? Turn your palms upwards for this portion, thanking him for the forgiveness and provision he has offered. Feel free to continue switching between these positions as needed.

Related Passages: Romans 8:34, Hebrews 7:24-26

Closing Prayer:

Jesus, thank you for being our advocate. By your loss, by your pain, by your death – you righted our wrongs. We are set free, not because you felt guilty or we forced your hand, but because you are a Father who loves the lost. You spoke, and we are clean. You forgave, and we became part of your family. Help me to surrender my pride – my striving to be enough – and to instead live in your righteousness today. Amen.

What are you calling me to release?

_____

_____

_____

_____

_____

_____

_____

_____

_____

_____

_____

_____

_____

What are you inviting me to receive?

_____

_____

_____

_____

_____

_____

_____

_____

_____

_____

_____

_____

_____

Know, Obey, Confess, Give Thanks
– Caitlyn Edwards –

Pause:

How is your heart doing today?

Are you feeling anxious, frustrated, or tired? Maybe excited or experiencing a fresh joy? Is there something weighing on your heart or causing you to feel distracted? Maybe sitting right here right now is a challenge. Take some time to acknowledge before the Lord where your heart is today.

Wherever you are, I am glad you are here. Because wherever your heart is at, this book of 1 John is an invitation to engage with the Eternal Word of Life; apart from him, there is no life.

Centering Prayer:

Father, thank you for your daily invitation into relationship with you as your beloved child. Help me to engage with your Word today with my whole self – heart, soul, mind, and strength.

Prayer Practice:

Read through 1 John 2. As you read, ask God these four questions (feel free to do it conversationally or journal it on the next page):

1. What truth do you want me to know?
2. What command do I need to obey?
3. What sin do I need to confess?
4. What gift or promise can I thank you for?

Closing Prayer:

Jesus, thank you for being my Advocate before the Father and atoning sacrifice for my sins. In you I have forgiveness, not because of my own righteousness or faithfulness, but because of yours. Thank you for setting for me an example of walking in love and in obedience to the Father. By your grace and by your strength, help me to abide in you and hold tightly to the truth of the gospel. Today, may you be my first love. Amen.

What truth do you want me to know?

_____

_____

_____

_____

_____

_____

_____

_____

_____

_____

_____

_____

_____

What command do I need to obey?

_____

_____

_____

_____

_____

_____

_____

_____

_____

_____

_____

_____

What sin do I need to confess?

_____

_____

_____

_____

_____

_____

_____

_____

_____

_____

_____

_____

What gift or promise can I thank you for?

_____

_____

_____

_____

_____

_____

_____

_____

_____

_____

_____

_____

_____

Study
– Jessica Skiles –

Pause:

Breathe in. Breathe out. Breathe in. Breathe out. In the middle of our hectic lives and culture, finding stillness seems like water slipping right through our fingers. However, true peace is not an achievement – it is a gift. It's the love of God, settling into furthest corners of our hearts: a deep understanding that we are *known* and we are *loved* by a perfect Father.

I want to encourage you to set your timer for two minutes today. Focus on your breathing – deep and slow. Close your eyes and *rest* in his presence. God has invited you to release your striving; you no longer have to prove you are good enough to him. You are accepted and invited as a daughter to come and be with him.

Opening Prayer:

Jesus, please open my eyes and my heart. Draw my attention to what you want me to see and guide my heart to obey. I am yours.

Study:

In 1 John 2, John draws a clear distinction between a life lived *with* God and a life lived apart from him. Over the next several minutes, read 1 John 2 and write down these comparisons that you see. What has God extended to you in this chapter? What does he warn against?

Characteristics of Life *with* God	Characteristics of Life *Apart* from God

In place of sin, death, and separation – God has offered us forgiveness, hope, and light. With this dichotomy in mind, read through verses 18-27 again. How does this context help explain the urgency of John's words here?

_____

_____

_____

_____

_____

_____

_____

_____

_____

Spend the next couple of minutes discussing your thoughts with the Lord. Are you grateful for the gifts he has extended to you? Praise him for those things! Do you feel the weight of sin and darkness on your shoulders? Offer that up to him. Ask for his truth to overcome lies that keep entangling you.

Closing Prayer:

Jesus, thank you for inviting us to come close to you. You have offered us life beyond our wildest dreams – we are intertwined with perfect love. We believe that you have placed your Spirit in us, prompting and guiding us into your truth. Help us to listen, Father! Help us to cling to you, break down the lies of the enemy and the wisdom of this world. We trust you, God. Help us to lean into your love every day, pressing into the things we know to be true. Amen.

Truth, Lies, and Declaration
– Rhonda Hayward –

Pause:

After asking God for guidance to write this devotional, I looked up and saw a plaque on my kitchen wall with these words, "Live by grace, not perfection". The passage in 1 John that we are studying today exhorts us not to sin, but to instead obey God's ways. However, God knows we won't do that perfectly. And that is where God's love and grace enter. Are there any other overcoming legalists or perfectionists out there like me? Take heart and soak up the incredible grace and hope of this passage.

Centering Prayer:

I thank you Jesus, My Advocate and Defender, for your love and grace. Give me your Spirit of wisdom and revelation right now to better understand and embrace your forgiveness and grace in my life. Reveal to me any lies I have been believing and help me replace that with your truth. Thank you! In Jesus' Saving Name, Amen!

Truth, Lies, And Declaration:

Read slowly through 1 John 1:5-2:2 two or three times. Ask God's Spirit to highlight any truth He wants you to claim. Write that truth out in your journal.

> **Example Truth**:
>
> ■ God will forgive me every time I sin (1 John 1:9)
>
> ■ I (and others) want to obey you, but nevertheless, we will mess up and sin. Jesus as my Advocate stands before the Father and declares that his shed blood takes away our sins (1 John 2:1-2).

Now, ask God's Spirit to show you any lie you are believing that opposes that truth. Renounce and repent of that lie and replace it with the truth God has shown you.

> **Example Lies:**
>
> ■ God won't/can't forgive me of *this:* _____ " (fill in the blank)
>
> ■ "Daddy-God, I confess I have believed the lie that there are some sins you won't forgive or sins I think I've committed one too many times for you to forgive. I repent of and renounce that lie. I now declare and own the truth that when I confess my sin, any sin, you forgive me, every time. Thank you for your abounding grace!"

Write a declaration based on the truth God showed you. Put it as a reminder on your phone or on an index card or sticky note in a visible place. Commit to declaring that truth out loud daily until it becomes part of your spiritual DNA. Add a Scripture reference to back up that declaration. The enemy cannot refute us when we simply state, "It is *written!*"

Example Declaration:

- I declare the truth that when I confess my sin, any sin, you forgive me, every time. Thank you for your abounding grace! (1 John 1:9)

- I declare the truth that though I want to obey you, I sometimes will mess up and sin. Thank you, Jesus, that you stand in heaven as my Advocate and declare me righteous to the Father because of your shed blood (1 John 2:1-2). Thank you for your amazing grace!

Closing Prayer:

Daddy-God, whenever I feel accused and condemned because of my sin, help me to be quicker to recognize the lies under those feelings. I commit to renouncing those lies and will instead declare and own your truth. I thank you for your unfailing love, grace and forgiveness! I love you, Jesus. Amen!

What truth do you want me to see in this chapter?

_____
_____
_____
_____
_____
_____
_____
_____

Are there any lies that I have been believing that oppose this truth?

_____
_____
_____
_____
_____
_____
_____

What declaration of truth do you have for me today?

_____
_____
_____
_____
_____
_____
_____

Lectio Divina
– Jessica Skiles –

Pause:

"Be still and know that I am God."
– Psalm 46:10

Throughout his entire book, John is inviting this group of believers to press into the things they know to be true. In most cases, he isn't giving them "new information" – they've all experienced the gospel and are well – versed in the golden rule. However, John calls them to *lean deeply* into this love: to draw in even closer to the God they've already come to know.

So as we begin, use this as a chance to *lean in.* Close your eyes and take in a deep breath, thinking on the phrase: *"Be still and know".* As you release that breath, exhale the remainder of the verse: *"that I am God."* Remember the ways that God has shown Himself to you and continue to repeat this process for two minutes.

Opening Prayer:

Jesus, I believe you are who you have claimed to be. You are my righteousness, you are my salvation, you are my kind and attentive Father. You go before me in power, you walk beside me in kindness. I will trust you when you say that you have drawn near to me; give me an open heart to receive your love and presence today.

Lectio Divina:

Settle into a position that will help you focus – this could be sitting at the dining table, maybe kneeling in your bedroom. Turn to 1 John 2:12-17, opening your hands in a posture ready to *receive* from God. Ask him to guide you through these next four steps.

1. Read 1 John 2:12-17 once slowly. Ask God to draw your attention to a *word* or a *phrase*, and then write it down.

2. Read the same passage a second time. What *image* comes to mind? Draw or describe what you see and take note of various *memories* and *emotions* that rise to the surface during this time.

3. Read it through a third time. What *meaning* is God highlighting for you in this phrase or passage? Allow yourself to freely engage with God in conversation about the things he is showing you. Ask questions, sing a song, or maybe just sit quietly and ponder what he has said in this text.

4. Finally, read through this one more time, slowly. Rest in his presence and allow this text to wash over you as you prepare to move forward into your day.

Closing Prayer:

Father, thank you for being a God who draws us in close. You have given us forgiveness, victory, and belonging; in your presence, we find everything we need. Thank you for speaking to me today. Help me to remain in you. Amen.

Word or Phrase

Image

How are you inviting me to respond?

_____

_____

_____

_____

_____

_____

_____

_____

_____

_____

_____

_____

_____

_____

_____

_____

_____

_____

_____

_____

_____

_____

_____

_____

_____

Obedience

– Jessica Skiles –

Pause:

At every turn, John tells us our Christian walk is known by our active relationship with God and his people. It's not just a sentiment – it's our time, energy, possessions and priorities![13] Our lives are overlapped in a way that is tangible, powerful, and transforming.[14]

Over the next two minutes, ask God to open your heart to this kind of vulnerability. Visualize yourself having a conversation with God about what it may look like for you to draw near to him and to your Christian family.

Opening Prayer:

Jesus, would you give me an open heart to receive difficult things from you today? Would you teach me what it truly looks like to love your people, and give me the strength and desire to follow through?

Obedience:

Read 1 John 2:1-11. Many times, it can be the people who are closest to us – the people we should be able to trust the most – who cause us the deepest wounds. In the realest sense, Jesus knows this pain.[2] When we allow these wounds to fester, however, they produce resentment and mistrust – blinding us to the light and life God offers. In an effort to protect ourselves, we shut out others and eventually God himself.

Would you be willing to share that pain with your Father? Find a quiet place (preferably outside) and open your hands before God. Who

---

2. John 13:18-38

are you feeling wounded by? Say each of these names aloud, and as you speak, release those people and situations to him. Know that God is present and allow his Spirit to minister to you in this process.

Closing Prayer:

God, I'm tired of being blinded by my bitterness. I'm tired of holding these seeds of unforgiveness in my heart, but I don't have the strength to let go of them on my own. Would you dig them out? I know you're offering me a closeness – a whole new realm of living – that I can't step into until I let these things go. Jesus, you're reminding me that I've been forgiven – not because I earned it, but on account of your name. You restored our relationship. You brought me into vibrant and eternal life. Please work in me so that I can extend that same forgiveness to my brothers and sisters. Amen.

Art
– Jessica Skiles –

Pause:

I recently watched a video of a man with down's syndrome reunited with his eighty-eight-year-old father. For decades, this father had been his caregiver and constant companion. Although only separated for a week, the joy and embrace of their reunion was overwhelming. The son threw himself into his father's arms as the father's eyes glimmered with deep tenderness and affection. This son was the apple of his eye.

When I read 1 John 2:13, I think of this moment. I think of a love that runs long and deep – of a father who has proven himself faithful every single time. It's the contentment of a child whose home and security are truly found in that love. The years have only proven that he is safe and treasured. He knows that he won't be turned away.

For the next two minutes, I want you to pause and reflect on that kind of love. Breathe deeply and ask God to open your heart to receive it.

Opening Prayer:

Father, thank you for drawing me close. Help me to lean into your love and learn from you today.

Short Story:

Today's art expression is *story*: a powerful tool that invites us to experientially step into the text. It moves us from *observers* to *participators*, inviting us to interact with its thoughts, emotions, and experiences.

As we begin, reflect for a moment on the vivid imagery of 1 John

2:28-3:3. What image begins to form in your mind? Maybe words like "trust, safety, home" or the name of a loved one (a parent, friend you really respect, your own kids that you adore, etc.) – write these down. Flesh these out into a paragraph or two, describing what you imagine or have experienced as close, sacrificial love between two people.

Now read through 1 John 2:28-3:3 again. Ask God, "what do you want me to see?" as you reflect on these questions.

- What truth about God does this point me to?
- What truth about my identity in Christ does this remind me of?
- What truth about the Church does this help me understand?

Closing Prayer:

Father, thank you for calling me your child – for drawing me in, for giving me hope. I am chosen; I belong to a family. Help me to lean into your love! Let it transform my anxiety into peace, my striving into rest. I trust you, help me to trust you more. Amen.

What truth about God does this point me to?

_____

_____

_____

_____

_____

_____

_____

_____

What truth about my identity in Christ does this remind me of?

_____

_____

_____

_____

_____

_____

_____

_____

What truth about the Church does this help me understand?

_____

_____

_____

_____

_____

_____

_____

_____

WEEK 3

1 John 3:1-24

[1] See what great love the Father has lavished on us, that we should be called children of God! And that is what we are! The reason the world does not know us is that it did not know him. [2] Dear friends, now we are children of God, and what we will be has not yet been made known. But we know that when Christ appears, we shall be like him, for we shall see him as he is. [3] All who have this hope in him purify themselves, just as he is pure.

[4] Everyone who sins breaks the law; in fact, sin is lawlessness. [5] But you know that he appeared so that he might take away our sins. And in him is no sin. [6] No one who lives in him keeps on sinning. No one who continues to sin has either seen him or known him.

[7] Dear children, do not let anyone lead you astray. The one who does what is right is righteous, just as he is righteous. [8] The one who does what is sinful is of the devil, because the devil has been sinning from the beginning. The reason the Son of God appeared was to destroy the devil's work. [9] No one who is born of God will continue to sin, because God's seed remains in them; they cannot go on sinning, because they have been born of God. [10] This is how we know who the children of God are and who the children of the devil are: Anyone who does not do what is right is not God's child, nor is anyone who does not love their brother and sister.

[11] For this is the message you heard from the beginning: We should love one another. [12] Do not be like Cain, who belonged to the evil one and murdered his brother. And why did he murder him? Because his own actions were evil and his brother's were righteous. [13] Do not be surprised, my brothers and sisters, if the world hates you. [14] We know that we have passed from death to life, because

we love each other. Anyone who does not love remains in death. [15] Anyone who hates a brother or sister is a murderer, and you know that no murderer has eternal life residing in him.

[16] This is how we know what love is: Jesus Christ laid down his life for us. And we ought to lay down our lives for our brothers and sisters. [17] If anyone has material possessions and sees a brother or sister in need but has no pity on them, how can the love of God be in that person? [18] Dear children, let us not love with words or speech but with actions and in truth.

[19] This is how we know that we belong to the truth and how we set our hearts at rest in his presence: [20] If our hearts condemn us, we know that God is greater than our hearts, and he knows everything. [21] Dear friends, if our hearts do not condemn us, we have confidence before God [22] and receive from him anything we ask, because we keep his commands and do what pleases him. [23] And this is his command: to believe in the name of his Son, Jesus Christ, and to love one another as he commanded us. [24] The one who keeps God's commands lives in him, and he in them. And this is how we know that he lives in us: We know it by the Spirit he gave us.

Palms Up, Palms Down
– Jessica Skiles –

Pause:

"Jesus came to take away our sins."
– 1 John 3:5 (NLT)

Sometimes, I think we forget why Jesus came. Yes, Jesus came to heal, to preach, to show God's love to us. He came to die and raise to life, even. But do you remember that he came with intention – with a real solution for *your* sin problem? Before we get caught in the "But I's," or "well, maybe's," take a moment to soak in that truth.

Close your eyes and take in some long, slow breaths. As you inhale, breathe in the first phrase of that verse: *"Jesus came."* Then exhale the remainder: *"to take away our sins."* Set a timer for two minutes and continue to repeat this process.

Opening Prayer:

Jesus, thank you for taking away our sins when we had no power to do it ourselves. I love you and thank you. Please open my heart to receive what you have to say to me today.

Prayer Practice:

1 John is a book marked by contrast – comparing a life of purity in Christ and a life of sin apart from him. As you read through the comparisons of 1 John 3:2-10, hold your hands out in front of you and ask the Spirit these two questions.

1. *"What are you asking me to release?"* Turn your palms downward and confess to him your need. As you read, do you recognize any lies you've been believing, sins you've been holding onto, or temptations you don't know how to let go of? Ask him to help you release those things.

2. *"What are you inviting me to receive?"* Flip your palms upwards, thanking him for the things you see extended to you in this passage (purity, adoption, etc.). Are you struggling to accept his forgiveness or live in his way? Ask for his help in receiving it!

Feel free to continue switching between these positions as many times as needed.

Closing Prayer:

Jesus, thank you for offering me hope: that in your presence, I truly am purified. Help me to know your love more deeply – releasing the sin I have held so tightly and walking in your way. I love you, thank you for choosing me as your child. Amen.

What are you calling me to release?

_____

_____

_____

_____

_____

_____

_____

_____

_____

_____

_____

_____

_____

_____

What are you inviting me to receive?

_____

_____

_____

_____

_____

_____

_____

_____

_____

_____

_____

_____

_____

_____

Know, Obey, Confess, Give Thanks
– Kim McIntire –

Pause:

Before you approach God's Word, reflect on these questions as a meditation.

- *What is the greatest expression of human love you have ever experienced?*

- *Who expressed this love toward you?*

- *In what ways is their love expressed?*

- *How does receiving this love impact your life as an individual?*

As you approach this passage today meditate on the love that God has lavished upon you . . . a love that allows you to be a child of God!

Opening Prayer:

Father God, in Jesus' name and through the power of your Holy Spirit, open my heart, mind, and spirit to hear your voice speaking through your Word. I ask you to guide my thoughts and silence all distractions. I pray to fully receive and live out the message of truth that you have for me today. I ask you to take this truth and transform me by your Holy Spirit.

Prayer Practice:

Read 1 John 3 and ask yourself the following questions that engage your mind, heart, and spirit. *Settle* yourself in the presence of the Lord.

Prepare to *receive* from him truth that will grow and transform you.

"What truth do you want me to know?"
The Father invites us to know truth specific from this passage.

"What command do I need to obey? What sin do I need to confess?"
He wants to call us to new levels of obedience and
deeper places of confession through time in his Word.

"What gift or promise can I thank you for?"
He has given us so much to thank him for as we receive today.
Allow his Spirit to take you to these places as you commune with him.

God has spoken to you through his Word. How will you respond to what he has spoken to your heart today?

Closing Prayer:

Father God, For the deep love you lavish upon me, I thank you. For calling me your child, I praise you. Help me to know that I am in you and being purified daily because my hope is in you. You destroyed the devil's works and have won! The truth that I am your child gives me confidence that I can obey you. Your seed remains in me! I confess, Lord, there are times I lose sight of what I have received from you. Forgive me, Lord. Help me to keep your commands, and to love others. At times, both are a struggle! Lord, I know that I live in you, and you live in me. Thank you. Grow these truths in my heart, I pray. In Jesus' name, Amen.

What truth do you want me to know?

_____

_____

_____

_____

_____

_____

_____

_____

_____

_____

_____

_____

_____

_____

What command do I need to obey?

_____

_____

_____

_____

_____

_____

_____

_____

_____

_____

_____

_____

_____

_____

What sin do I need to confess?

_____
_____
_____
_____
_____
_____
_____
_____
_____
_____

What gift or promise can I thank you for?

_____
_____
_____
_____
_____
_____
_____
_____
_____
_____
_____

Study
– Alexandria M. Brazle –

Pause:

This whole chapter hones in on what it means to love and how we know what love even looks like. How would we know if it were not shown to us first? But it also helps us to see who we are in God's eyes and how we can live in truth.

Take a breath and welcome God into this study time. Acknowledge that he's already been with you. Breath prayers have been utilized by believers for hundreds of years and are such a lovely way to ground ourselves in truth at any time. Try this one from Psalm 103:4-5 before jumping in today.

Inhale*: You surround me with love*

Exhale*: and tender mercies.*

Opening Prayer:

Jesus, you are ever present and always good. Show me what it means to love like you, and to be loved by you. I am waiting and open to learn.

Study:

1 John 3 is filled with an abundance of the truth of being God's beloved children and how adored we are. John tells us how we know what love is. Read verses 16-18. How do we know what love is? How can we do the same for others?

_____

_____

_____

Sometimes it can be helpful to look at cross-references in the Bible to get a well-rounded idea of a passage said in a different way. Read James 2:16-17. What do you think God's heart is for us to love in action and how does this show the love that he has shown us?

_____

_____

_____

_____

_____

Slowly read verses 1 John 3:19-22. How do you feel as you read these kind and loving verses? Do you feel at ease? Seen? Follow up with a reading from Hebrews 4:15-16. We are able to come to God's throne with **boldness,** or confidence. We receive mercy and he hears our hearts and prayers. John 15:7 also says, "If you abide in me, and my words abide in you, you will ask what you desire, and it shall be done for you." Is there anything that you would like to bring before him, knowing that you have full confidence and mercy covering you? What would you like him to know or ask for?

_____

_____

_____

_____

_____

Next, read through 1 John 3:19-24. This section is jam packed with how we can be assured that we walk in truth and that we know God truly and wholly. A cross-reference to verse 23 can be found in Mark 12:28-31. What does it mean to you when a section of Scripture, especially something that Jesus has said himself, has been quoted and taught throughout the New Testament?

_____

_____

_____

_____

_____

Closing Prayer:

Jesus, thank you for giving us mercy and grace. Thank you that you have shown us what it means to love others in action, and how you reassure our hearts that we are walking with you in truth. Your word comforts and guides, and we are thankful. Continue to show me how I can trust in you and love those around me as your hands and feet. Amen.

Truth, Lies, and Declaration
– Jessica Skiles –

Pause:

"If you hold to my teaching, you are really my disciples.
Then you will know the truth, and the truth will set you free"
– John 8:31-32

We are invited into a truth that is beautiful: not just to know, not just to hope for, but to plant our feet and *abide in*. A gospel truth that erases the shame of our past. A reality that offers genuine belonging for our loneliness. A tapping into the Holy Spirit who empowers us to *love* when it takes all we can muster just to get out of bed in the morning. A truth that is ever-more powerful than our fears and doubts because it is rooted in the *reality* of who God has revealed himself to be.

For the next two minutes, I want to invite you to release to the Lord whatever mental battle you may be in. As you breathe in deep, ask for his *truth* to wash over you and take root in your heart.

Opening Prayer:

Jesus, I need your word to take root and transform my thinking. Please break down the lies that I have been believing and reorient my heart around what is true. I am listening.

Truth, Lies, And Declaration:

Allow yourself some time for this exercise today – to drink it in slowly, rather than trying to absorb as much and as quickly as possible. Maybe this means closing the door, putting the phone away, setting a

87

timer – whatever would allow you to settle in and *listen*. Ask God to guide you through these steps as you read through 1 John 3.

Truth: *"Father, what truth do you want me to see in this chapter?"* As you read, write down the truths that stand out to you.

Lies: *"Are there any lies that I have been believing that oppose this truth?"* Renounce these and replace them with the truth that God just showed you.

Declaration: Write down a declaration and read it to yourself often throughout the week.

Closing Prayer:

Jesus, thank you for showing yourself to me. Please give me the strength to lean into your truth this week. Lead my thoughts, emotions, and attitudes into submission of your truth. I love you and I trust you. Amen.

What truth do you want me to see in this chapter?

_____

_____

_____

_____

_____

_____

_____

_____

Are there any lies that I have been believing that oppose this truth?

_____

_____

_____

_____

_____

_____

_____

_____

What declaration of truth do you have for me today?

_____

_____

_____

_____

_____

_____

_____

_____

Lectio Divina
– Jessica Skiles –

Pause:

Breathe in. Breathe out. Come and rest in the presence of your Father. As you close your eyes, visualize yourself releasing the weight you've been carrying on your shoulders. Allow the noise in your mind to fall silent and breathe deeply for the next two minutes.

Opening Prayer:

Jesus, you are so good to me . . . help me to lean into your love today. Give me ears to listen and heart that is open to what you have to say. I am listening.

Lectio Divina:

Settle into whatever posture seems most natural to you – this could be on your knees, out on your porch, or even snuggled up on your couch. Open your Bible to 1 John 3:4-10 (or pull up an audio version on your phone) and *breathe*. Ask God to guide you through these next four steps.

1. Read 1 John 3:4-10 once slowly. Ask God to draw your attention to a *word* or a *phrase*, and then write it down.

2. Read the same passage a second time. What *image* comes to mind? What *emotions* or *experience* rise to the surface?

3. Read it through a third time. What *meaning* is God highlighting for you? How is he inviting you to *respond* to

what he is showing you? Allow yourself to freely interact with him as you ponder these things.

4.   Finally, read through this one more time, slowly. Rest in his presence and allow this text to wash over you.

Closing Prayer:

Jesus, thank you for taking away my sin and calling me your child. I get to be truly yours – cleansed, righteous, and loved – because you made it so. Thank you for choosing the cross. Help me to cling to you. I love you. Amen.

Word or Phrase

Image

How is God inviting you to respond?

Obedience
– Jessica Skiles –

Pause:

"Jesus Christ laid down his life for us."
– 1 John 3:16

Interwoven through every command and encouragement in this book, John reminds us that we are compelled by the deep, sacrificial love we've received. We confess, remembering that God has extended grace to us. We forgive, remembering how he has forgiven us. We love because he first loved us.

Take a couple minutes to think about the ways that God has first reached out to you. Close your eyes, breathe deeply, and visualize his faithfulness to you over the years. Do this for the next two minutes.

Opening Prayer:

Father God, give me eyes to see your hand at work, a grateful heart that remembers your faithfulness. I am yours, take and use everything I have and everything I am for your glory. I am listening. May your love compel me to obey.

Obedience:

Read slowly through 1 John 3:11-18. After doing this two or three times, hold your hands out in front of you and ask God, *"Father, who are some people in my life who are in need?"* As he brings different names to mind, lift them up to him in prayer. Express their needs to God, ask for his provision in those situations.

Once you have finished this, read through 1 John 3:14-18 once more. Hold out your hands to Him again and ask, *"Father, how do you want me to respond to these needs?"* Do your best to listen openly and genuinely, not trying to censor or shape what he tells you to do. Write these things down and make a plan of how you are going to do those things this week.

Closing Prayer:

Father, thank you for your kindness and generosity to me. You have shown up far more than I know and could have ever asked for – often providing by calling those around me to be generous with their time and resources. Please grow in me a compassionate heart. Give me ears to truly listen and strength to obey what you call me to do. I am listening. Amen.

Who are some people in my life who are in need?

_____

_____

_____

_____

_____

_____

_____

_____

How do you want me to respond to those needs?

_____

_____

_____

_____

_____

_____

_____

What are my next steps?

_____

_____

_____

_____

_____

_____

_____

Art
– Rhonda Hayward –

Pause:

They told me it would happen. And it has. I have fallen in love. With my firstborn grandchild. The photograph you see is one of little Callen and his daddy, Aaron. The photo has utterly captivated my heart. God keeps sweetly and persistently whispering that this is his heart and posture towards *me* . . . towards *you*. This picture brings to life the phrase "apple of my eye" which literally means being so close to someone that you can see your reflection in the pupil of their eye. And be assured that whether Callen is mad, sad or glad, we remain delighted with him. This is SO God's heart for *us* . . . times a billion! As we gaze on his face, we only see unchanging love and delight. 1 John 3:1 in the NIV talks about God "lavishing his love". Pause for a minute or two now to study this picture, asking God to reveal his Father's lavishing heart of love for *you*.

Opening Prayer:

Spirit of the Living God, you are overwhelming Love and Grace. Tune my ears now to hear your True Voice alone. Unveil Daddy-God's heart of unfailing love.

Prayer Practice:

Slowly read through 1 John 3:1-3 a few times. With that passage in mind, study again the picture of Aaron & Callen and answer these questions:

- God, what do you want me to see?

- What truth about God does this point me to?

- What truth about my identity in Christ does this remind me of?

- What truth about the Church does this help me understand?

Take some time to lift prayers of gratitude, confession, and intercession.

Closing Prayer:

Daddy-God, thank you for lavishing your love on me. For making me your forever child. This love is beyond my ability to fully grasp. Please grant me ever increasing revelation and understanding into your heart of love. I choose from this day forward to see you and myself only through your lens of lavish love. May that love then overflow into the lives of those around me. Amen.

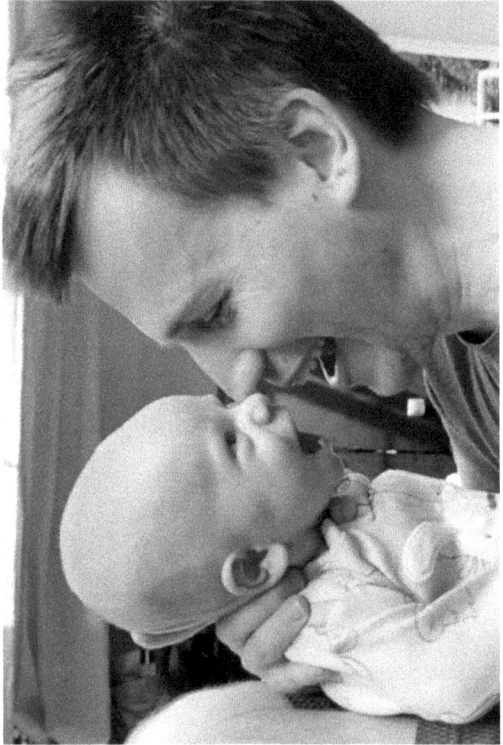

What truth about God does this point me to?

_____

_____

_____

_____

_____

_____

_____

What truth about my identity in Christ does this remind me of?

_____

_____

_____

_____

_____

_____

_____

What truth about the Church does this help me understand?

_____

_____

_____

_____

_____

_____

_____

WEEK 4

1 John 4:1-24

[1]Dear friends, do not believe every spirit, but test the spirits to see whether they are from God, because many false prophets have gone out into the world. [2]This is how you can recognize the Spirit of God: Every spirit that acknowledges that Jesus Christ has come in the flesh is from God, [3]but every spirit that does not acknowledge Jesus is not from God. This is the spirit of the antichrist, which you have heard is coming and even now is already in the world.

[4]You, dear children, are from God and have overcome them, because the one who is in you is greater than the one who is in the world. [5]They are from the world and therefore speak from the viewpoint of the world, and the world listens to them. [6]We are from God, and whoever knows God listens to us; but whoever is not from God does not listen to us. This is how we recognize the Spirit[a] of truth and the spirit of falsehood.[7]Dear friends, let us love one another, for love comes from God. Everyone who loves has been born of God and knows God. [8]Whoever does not love does not know God, because God is love. [9]This is how God showed his love among us: He sent his one and only Son into the world that we might live through him. [10]This is love: not that we loved God, but that he loved us and sent his Son as an atoning sacrifice for our sins. [11]Dear friends, since God so loved us, we also ought to love one another. [12]No one has ever seen God; but if we love one another, God lives in us and his love is made complete in us.

[13]This is how we know that we live in him and he in us: He has given us of his Spirit. [14]And we have seen and testify that the Father has sent his Son to be the Savior of the world. [15]If anyone acknowledges that Jesus is the Son of

God, God lives in them and they in God. [16] And so we know and rely on the love God has for us.

God is love. Whoever lives in love lives in God, and God in them. [17] This is how love is made complete among us so that we will have confidence on the day of judgment: In this world we are like Jesus. [18] There is no fear in love. But perfect love drives out fear, because fear has to do with punishment. The one who fears is not made perfect in love.

[19] We love because he first loved us. [20] Whoever claims to love God yet hates a brother or sister is a liar. For whoever does not love their brother and sister, whom they have seen, cannot love God, whom they have not seen. [21] And he has given us this command: Anyone who loves God must also love their brother and sister.

Palms Up, Palms Down
– Jessica Skiles –

Pause:

To the one who is coming into today frustrated, exhausted, and overwhelmed . . . you're not alone. As you step into this time–with whatever worries and to-do's you carry–join me in holding these out before the Father. Breathe in deeply and slowly.

"The one who is in you is greater than the one who is in the world."
–1 John 4:4

For the next two minutes, I invite you to do a breath prayer using this verse. As you inhale, breathe in the first half: *"The one who is in you is greater"*. As you release that breath, exhale the rest: *"than the one who is in the world."* Continue to repeat this process.

Opening Prayer:

Jesus, thank you for being greater than everything that I will face today. Help me to trust that promise. I love you. Open my heart to what you have to say to me today.

Prayer Practice:

In 1 John 3:23-4:6, John continues clarifying for this church what the people and message of God look like–contrasting it with those that reject God. Read these verses (out loud, if possible!), then hold your hands out before the Father and ask him these two questions:

1. *"What are you asking me to release?"* Turn your palms

downward and *listen*. What themes from this passage is he drawing you to? Is there doubt? Fear? A need to be respected by "the world?" Release these struggles to Him.

2. *"What are you inviting me to receive?"* Flip your palms upwards and, again, pause to truly listen. Is there a truth he wants you to hold onto? An attitude or act of obedience you need to take on? Ask for his help in receiving those things.

Continue to go between these two steps as many times as you need.

Closing Prayer:

Father, thank you for choosing to live inside of me. I am so grateful for your presence. Help me to live by your Spirit inside of me—may you guide every thought, word, and attitude. Grow in me a love for others and a desire to know you more deeply. I love you and I trust you. Amen.

What are you calling me to release?

_____

_____

_____

_____

_____

_____

_____

_____

_____

_____

_____

_____

What are you inviting me to receive?

_____

_____

_____

_____

_____

_____

_____

_____

_____

_____

_____

_____

Know, Obey, Confess, Give Thanks
– Jessica Skiles –

Pause:

Jesus, I am yours.

As you allow your mind and body to settle, use this phrase as a breath prayer to guide the next two minutes.

Inhale: *Jesus*

Exhale: *I am yours.*

As you do this, imagine the worries and weight you carry rolling off your shoulders, down your arms, out of your hands and into the hands of Jesus – the one who cares and can truly bear those burdens.

Opening Prayer:

Lord Jesus, I trust these things to you. Thank you for being with me in the deepest and truest sense. Help me to listen and trust what you have to say today.

Prayer Practice:

Read through 1 John 4 slowly (imagining yourself reading aloud can help with this). As you read, ask God these four questions:

1. What truth do you want me to know?
2. What command do I need to obey?
3. What sin do I need to confess?
4. What gift or promise can I thank you for?

Feel free to do this conversationally with God as you read, or to journal your prayers on the next page.

Closing Prayer:

Father, you said that perfect love drives out fear . . . thank you for loving me so deeply and fully. Help me to know and rely on your love today. Forgive me for the ways I have held onto bitterness and withheld kindness from those around me; please give me a heart that loves freely like yours. Amen.

What truth do you want me to know?

_____
_____
_____
_____
_____
_____
_____
_____
_____
_____
_____
_____
_____
_____

What command do I need to obey?

_____
_____
_____
_____
_____
_____
_____
_____
_____
_____
_____
_____
_____
_____

What sin do I need to confess?

_____

_____

_____

_____

_____

_____

_____

_____

_____

_____

_____

_____

What gift or promise can I thank you for?

_____

_____

_____

_____

_____

_____

_____

_____

_____

_____

_____

_____

Study
– Michelle Schaffer –

Pause:

As you come to the Father in prayer today, quiet yourself and still your heart, ready to receive whatever the Lord has for you.

As I take in deep breaths and long exhales, I answer the invitation to quiet myself at the feet of Jesus: inhaling his truth and exhaling any lies that hinder me from hearing his truth.

Take a couple minutes to sit in the joy of the mystery that comes with the silence. Focus on what truth and what love Jesus will speak to you today.

Opening Prayer:

Lord, I know you are truth and you are love. I ask for you to open my heart to receive those both today. Silence any noise, any distractions that would hinder me from hearing you at this moment. With open hands and open heart, I sit still to listen to your voice. As the sheep recognize the voice of their shepherd, may I also recognize the voice of my Father. May my thoughts, my actions, my words and my attitude be transformed by your word and by your Spirit. Renew, restore and redeem me today. All the glory, all the honor and all the praise be to you!

Study:

Agape or Apapaō means to love with action. The definition of this Greek word means *"to love, esteem, feel or manifest generous concern for, be faithful towards; to delight in, to set store upon."* We see this Greek word all throughout 1 John as John tells us about what true love looks like.

We see this true *agape* love exemplified in Jesus. Jesus' love for us was proven to us by his death and resurrection. 1 John 4: 10 says that the sending of God's son is what real love is, *"not that we have loved God but that he loved us."* But Jesus' death and resurrection weren't the only examples of love that he showed us. Jesus also lived with his people. God's love isn't only in death but in the life of Christ. Jesus not only came down as a human to come down to our level, but he sat with people, ate with people, taught and healed people. He especially did this with outcasts, with strangers, and especially with his enemies. His love came with actions seen through his life and – just how faith is not complete without works – love works the same way. We love others because of the faith we have in Jesus. If we love others well, we will know God well. Because he is love.

John 21 mentions another writing of John's where we see the Greek word *agape*. Jesus asks Peter twice if he has *agape* love for him and each time he responds with a yes, Jesus tells Peter to follow that love with action. That action was to show love to his lambs and his sheep, meaning His people. We can't love God if we don't love our brothers and sisters in Christ (1 John 4:20). It can be hard to love our family in Christ especially if one has wronged you, hurt you, or disagreed with you. But we know it's not impossible. We aren't held to our flesh when we know Christ (Rom. 8:9). And it's the love with which God fills our cup that helps us to pour our love to others.

Take time to pray and write down what the Spirit is telling you about loving others. What ways can we show the agape love of Christ? Write down the names of those you need to show unconditional love to.

Closing Prayer:

Jesus, grow in me an agape *love that is as sweet, merciful, and full of grace as your own. Help me to show love towards others without any condition, without any expectation but solely with the pureness of your own love. May my love for others be deprived of any stereotyping, any maliciousness, and any cruelty that is not of you. In times I don't know how to love, teach me Lord, and grow in me a love that is full of truth. May I know you deeper by the love that I not only show to you, but also to myself and especially to others, and may my love for people intensify the love I have for you. May all the love, glory, honor, and praise be unto you. Amen.*

Who do I need to show unconditional love to?

_____

_____

_____

_____

_____

_____

_____

_____

_____

_____

_____

_____

_____

_____

_____

_____

_____

_____

_____

_____

_____

_____

_____

_____

_____

_____

Truth, Lies, and Declaration
– Alexandria M. Brazle –

Pause:

> *How priceless is your unfailing love, O God!*
> *People take refuge in the shadow of your wings*
> *– Psalm 36:7*

We are able to bask in God's love that never fails, never wavers, and is always available for us to take refuge in. Settle in now with the knowledge that you are wholly loved and nothing can take this from you. That God invites us into His love to stay and rest, to live our lives in light of the knowledge that we are safe with him.

For the next minute, breathe in deeply that you are seen and loved, and breathe out any anxiety and mental struggles you may have today. Release your worries and struggles to the Father and open yourself to his *truth.*

Centering Prayer:

Jesus, transform my heart and mind to trust and believe that you are for me and love me. Reveal to me what lies I believe and replace them with your truth. Guide this time and allow me to rest in your love.

Truth, Lies, And Declaration:

Give yourself the physical and mental space to revel in this chapter. Let the Father's truth and heart for you wrap you in an embrace as you read this passage. Although it may be familiar, read slowly. Soak it in.

Truth: *"Father, what truth do you want me to see in this chapter?"* As you read, write down the truths that stand out to you. What makes your heart skip a beat or forces you to reread a certain verse?

Lies: *"Are there any lies that I have been believing that oppose this truth?"* Acknowledge what misconceptions you believe about God or about yourself. What pieces of yourself do you believe are unlovable? Write them down and release them to God. Let him tell you that you are loved.

Declaration: Write down a declaration from this chapter and put it in a place you'll see often. Write it on your phone, make it the background picture, put it near your kitchen sink.

Closing Prayer:

Jesus, thank you for your sacrifice so that I might know what true love is and experience it everyday. Help me to soak this truth in and really believe it for myself. Help me to accept that I am loved and wanted. Amen.

What truth do you want me to see in this chapter?

_____

_____

_____

_____

_____

_____

_____

_____

Are there any lies that I have been believing that oppose this truth?

_____

_____

_____

_____

_____

_____

_____

_____

What declaration of truth do you have for me today?

_____

_____

_____

_____

_____

_____

_____

_____

Lectio Divina
– Jessica Skiles –

Pause:

> *"It is impossible to love deeply without sacrifice."*
> *– Elisabeth Elliot[15]*

If you have ever worn the title of friend, wife, sister, mom . . . you know this to be true. Whether the price tag has been sleepless nights and dirty diapers or long phone calls and bridesmaid dresses, every meaningful relationship requires that we set aside our time, money, and priorities for someone else. John affirms this throughout his book and points us to the ultimate example of Jesus Christ (check out 1 John 4:10!).[16]

As you settle into this time, reflect on ways that you have tangibly received this kind of love from others. Allow the emotion of those experiences to wash over you. How do these experiences help you to better understand the sacrificial love you have received from God?

Opening Prayer:

Father, thank you for giving of yourself so generously. Grow in me a heart that reflects that love for others; help me to live by the Spirit you have placed inside of me. I am listening, I am yours.

Lectio Divina:

Breath in deeply, slowly. Open your Bible to 1 John 4:7-12 (or pull up an audio version on your phone). Ask God to guide you through these four movements.

1. Read 1 John 4:7-12 once slowly. Ask God to draw your attention to a *word* or a *phrase*, and then write it down.

2. Read the same passage a second time. What *image* comes to mind?[3] What *emotions* or *experience* rise to the surface?

3. Read it through a third time. What *meaning* is God highlighting for you? How is he inviting you to *respond* to what he is showing you? Allow yourself to freely interact with him as you ponder these things.

4. Finally, read through this one more time, slowly. Rest in his presence and allow this text to wash over you.

Closing Prayer:

Father, thank you for loving me first. Before I sought you – before I even knew I needed you – you reached out to me. You offered to pull me out of the mess I made. Thank you for the cross! Let the Gospel transform the way that I treat people, may your love flow through me to those around me. In Jesus' name, amen.

---

3. This is a chance to "step into" the scene. For example, maybe "atoning sacrifice" triggers an image of Jesus' crucifixion. Put yourself within that scene, asking yourself, *"What do I hear? What do I see? How do I engage with the things going on around me?"* Allow your senses to speak into your reading, not just your intellect!

Word or Phrase

Image

How is God inviting you to respond?

Obedience
– Danielle Wheeler –

Pause:

Today as you enter into prayerful silence, allow your body to relax into God's presence. Unclench your jaw. Release your shoulders. Relax the space between your eyebrows. Deeply inhale and exhale. Become aware of God's loving presence with you.

Opening Prayer:

Father . . .my Creator,

Jesus . . .my Savior,

Holy Spirit . . .my Indweller,

I enter into this space with you now.

Prayer Practice:

The disciple John, the author of 1 John, identified himself as "the one whom Jesus loved." His core identity was "the Beloved Disciple." Beloved is how he saw himself. Beloved is how he knew God saw him. John used a special word to describe this beloved relationship. It was perhaps his favorite word, the Greek word "μένω" – *meno´* (men'-o).

This is a difficult word to translate into English, thus it is translated as several different English words: to abide, to stay, to remain, to wait.

In the Old Testament we see the Hebrew word " שָׁכַן" – *shakan* (shaw-kan'). This word is translated into English with these words: to abide, to dwell, to settle down, to lie down, to live, to nest, to rest.

John the Beloved Disciple loved this rich, intimate concept of abiding. In John chapter 15, he uses the word *meno´* 11 times. In the books of 1 John and 2 John, he uses the word 27 times.

Read 1 John 4: 12-16 and see if you can find the 6 times in this short passage where he used the word *meno.´* Read the passage again slowly.

Do you see the miracle and mystery here? The God of the universe *abides in you.* God remains in you, stays in you, waits in you, lives in you, settles down in you, lies down in you, nests in you, and rests in you. And he invites you to do the same in him.

John paints a picture of abiding in Revelation 3:20, *"Here I am! I stand at the door and knock. If anyone hears my voice and opens the door, I will come in and eat with that person, and they with me."*

Pause now with your eyes closed. Imagine Jesus knocking at the door to the inner sanctuary of your soul.

Use these questions to guide an imaginative prayer:

- *What do you feel when you hear his knock?*
- *What is your response?*
- *When you open the door, what do you see?*
- *What is Jesus' posture toward you?*
- *How do you respond?*
- *What is it like for him to come in and eat with you?*

Enter that picture with all the senses of your imagination.
Abide with him.

Closing Prayer:

Use John 15:4 as a breath prayer.

Inhale: *Abide in me,*

Exhale: *and I in you.*

Repeat several times, extending it as an invitation to God, and receiving it as an invitation from him. Soak in the richness of the word "abide." Carry the breath prayer with you into your day.

Art
– Rhonda Hayward –

Pause:

> *"God showed how much He loved us by sending*
> *His one and only Son into the world."*
> *– 1 John 4:9*

Oh. How. He LOVES! And knowing we are loved . . . *like that .
. .* changes *everything*! How could knowing the depths of God's love
change your outlook on life? We read that *"perfect love casts out fear"*.
Yes, knowing *He* loves me like *that* changes *everything*. When I know I
am loved, it makes me brave.

Opening Prayer:

*Daddy, your love is mind-boggling! Beyond my understanding. As I
read these verses, grant me supernatural grace to know "how wide and
long and high and deep is the love of God that passes understanding".
Because knowing that love will change everything.*

Prayer Practice:

Slowly read through 1 John 4:9-19 two or three times. With that
passage in mind, study "The Bridal Warrior" painting and answer these
questions:

- ■ God, what do you want me to see?
- ■ What truth about God does this point me to?
- ■ What truth about my identity in Christ does this remind me of?
- ■ What truth about the Church does this help me understand?

Take some time to lift prayers of gratitude, confession, and intercession.

Closing Prayer:

Oh Daddy-God! You ARE Love! Wash me again and again with ever increasing revelation of your love until all fear is GONE! Compelled by that love, I will fall on my face in worship and then run, not walk, to share this too-good-to-keep-to-myself love with all who live in a love-drought world. You are SO good! I love you! Amen.

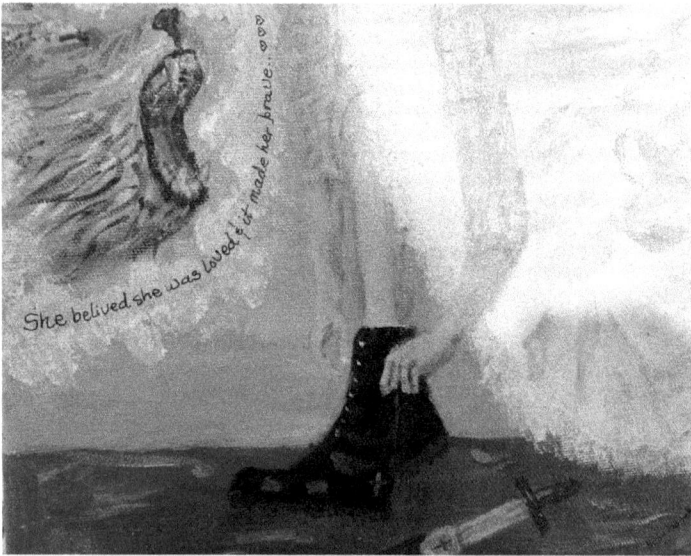

Just before sending off my painting for this devo, I discovered I had misspelled the word: "believed". I was dismayed and very embarrassed at first, but God is teaching me to pause and ask for HIS perspective. And as I did, I saw his smile, his wink and recognized his sense of humor because this was an illustration within the illustration of the very topic at hand . . . God's love and grace that dispels all fear and makes us brave! We do not have to be perfect because we are perfectly loved!

What truth about God does this point me to?

_____

_____

_____

_____

_____

_____

_____

_____

What truth about my identity in Christ does this remind me of?

_____

_____

_____

_____

_____

_____

_____

_____

What truth about the Church does this help me understand?

_____

_____

_____

_____

_____

_____

_____

_____

WEEK 5

1 John 5:1-21

¹Everyone who believes that Jesus is the Christ is born of God, and everyone who loves the father loves his child as well. ² This is how we know that we love the children of God: by loving God and carrying out his commands. ³ In fact, this is love for God: to keep his commands. And his commands are not burdensome, ⁴ for everyone born of God overcomes the world. This is the victory that has overcome the world, even our faith. ⁵ Who is it that overcomes the world? Only the one who believes that Jesus is the Son of God.

⁶ This is the one who came by water and blood – Jesus Christ. He did not come by water only, but by water and blood. And it is the Spirit who testifies, because the Spirit is the truth. ⁷ For there are three that testify: ⁸ the Spirit, the water and the blood; and the three are in agreement. ⁹ We accept human testimony, but God's testimony is greater because it is the testimony of God, which he has given about his Son. ¹⁰ Whoever believes in the Son of God accepts this testimony. Whoever does not believe God has made him out to be a liar, because they have not believed the testimony God has given about his Son. ¹¹ And this is the testimony: God has given us eternal life, and this life is in his Son. ¹² Whoever has the Son has life; whoever does not have the Son of God does not have life.

¹³ I write these things to you who believe in the name of the Son of God so that you may know that you have eternal life. ¹⁴ This is the confidence we have in approaching God: that if we ask anything according to his will, he hears us. ¹⁵ And if we know that he hears us – whatever we ask – we know that we have what we asked of him.

¹⁶ If you see any brother or sister commit a sin that does not lead to death,

you should pray and God will give them life. I refer to those whose sin does not lead to death. There is a sin that leads to death. I am not saying that you should pray about that. [17] All wrongdoing is sin, and there is sin that does not lead to death.

[18] We know that anyone born of God does not continue to sin; the One who was born of God keeps them safe, and the evil one cannot harm them. [19] We know that we are children of God, and that the whole world is under the control of the evil one. [20] We know also that the Son of God has come and has given us understanding, so that we may know him who is true. And we are in him who is true by being in his Son Jesus Christ. He is the true God and eternal life.

[21] Dear children, keep yourselves from idols.

Palms Up, Palms Down
– Jessica Skiles –

Pause:

Sometimes when I pray, it feels like I'm spending so much energy trying to bar the door of distractions–bracing it just long enough for a few verses or a short prayer before they come barging back in. If this is you today, I invite you to stop fighting. Open the door, and instead visualize yourself holding each of those things up before God. Are you worried about finances? Is your stomach in tangles from an argument last night? Breathe deeply, look into his face, and lift up each one of those situations to him. Visualize yourself leaving those things in his hands.

Opening Prayer:

Jesus, thank you for seeing me in my need. I trust these things to you, help me to leave them in your hands. Open my heart to receive your truth and presence today.

Prayer Practice:

Read through 1 John 5 slowly, allowing yourself to linger on any words that may catch your eye. As you read, ask these two questions.

1. *"What are you asking me to release?"* Turn your palms downward and *listen*. Share with God any sins, doubts, or fears that rise to the surface when reading.

2. *"What are you inviting me to receive?"* Flip your palms upwards and, again, pause to truly listen. What truth or attitude is he inviting you to take hold of? What blessing has

he extended to you?

Allow the text to spark confession, gratitude, and requests as you continue to change between these two positions.

Closing Prayer:

Father, thank you for making me your child . . . you have loved me with a love that is deeper than I will ever understand. Thank you for listening to my prayers, for offering me victory, for bringing me into life. Please teach me to love those around me and tear down these idols in my heart – I want my trust to be in you alone. Amen.

What are you calling me to release?

_____

_____

_____

_____

_____

_____

_____

_____

_____

_____

_____

_____

_____

What are you inviting me to receive?

_____

_____

_____

_____

_____

_____

_____

_____

_____

_____

_____

_____

_____

Know, Obey, Confess, Give Thanks
– Kim McIntire –

Pause:

Ask yourself this question as you approach God's Word today: *Does my relationship with Father God reflect a life of obedience and surrender?*

Meditate on the following phrase: *Father, I love you. I desire to obey and surrender to you.*

Opening Prayer:

Father, I desire to live in deep relationship with you. I know authentic love is connected to obedience. Reveal truth to my spirit as I read your Word now. What do you want me to know, Father? What areas of my life are you calling me into deeper levels of obedience? Is there sin in my heart that you want to cleanse me from? What truth can I specifically thank you for today?

Prayer Practice:

Read through 1 John 1 slowly, asking God these questions as you go:

1. What truth do you want me to know?
2. What command do I need to obey?
3. What sin do I need to confess?
4. What gift or promise can I thank you for?

Closing Prayer:

Lord, what I know clearly from this passage is that to love you is to

139

obey you. Your commands are not a heavy burden: they are the freedom my heart craves. When I love and obey you, I experience victory over sin that can come only from your presence and Holy Spirit. This is true victory born of faith, and it is only experienced through obedience to you. Yet I confess this is my greatest struggle! May I not silence your voice by neglecting your Word and presence. Help me live surrendered to your authority! In doing so, I am transformed as you renew my mind. My prayer is my love for you grows deeper and I'm filled by the Holy Spirit with a desire to obey that surpasses my desire for selfish gain. For the gift of your love, authority, the Holy Spirit, and the blood of Jesus – I thank you, my Lord. Help me to abide in you and receive all that you have for my heart as I continually seek your presence. Amen.

What truth do you want me to know?

_____

_____

_____

_____

_____

_____

_____

_____

_____

_____

_____

_____

_____

What command do I need to obey?

_____

_____

_____

_____

_____

_____

_____

_____

_____

_____

_____

_____

What sin do I need to confess?

_____
_____
_____
_____
_____
_____
_____
_____
_____
_____
_____

What gift or promise can I thank you for?

_____
_____
_____
_____
_____
_____
_____
_____
_____
_____
_____
_____

Study
– Jessica Skiles –

Pause:

I was once told by a professor that, in any given interaction, there are two basic questions we are all silently asking: *"Do you care about me?"* and *"Can I trust you?"* Whether we admit it or not, I believe these are also the questions we ask when approaching God.

As we prepare to unpack the truth surrounding these questions, take a couple of minutes to pause. Release the stress in your neck, shoulders, and hands. Focus your attention on your breathing–keeping it deep and slow.

Opening Prayer:

Holy Spirit, please open my heart to receive your truth today. Help me to truly listen with quietness and trust as I study your Word. I am yours.

Study:

Read 1 John 5:6-12 slowly, jotting down any words that seem significant, repeated, or confusing. When reading an unclear passage, it is helpful to read it in light of other related passages. Ask yourself: *"Does this remind me of/refer to other parts of Scripture?"* Google is your friend on this! Type in "cross references for 1 John 5:6-12" and wander the Scripture rabbit trails it leads you down. What common ideas and truths keep popping up?

_____

_____

_____
_____
_____
_____

Many scholars think John is alluding to Jesus' baptism (water), crucifixion (blood), and the Holy Spirit anointing on believers (Spirit). These represent the whole of Jesus' time on earth and distinguish Him as God *and* man – pushing back *hard* against the message of the false teachers.[17] They testify that His sacrifice was *real* and *exactly* what we needed.

Can I trust you? Do you care about me?

Read Matthew 3:16-17, John 19:32-37, 1 Peter 2:23-25, and Romans 8:15-17 and interact with God on how these passages might answer those two questions.

_____
_____
_____
_____
_____
_____

Closing Prayer:
Thank you that the answer to these questions is a resounding YES in Christ. I can trust the promises you make; you have proven on the cross that your love is sacrificial, deep and unwavering. You didn't owe us your presence, but you gave it. You didn't have to give so many clear

signs of your gospel plan, but you did. You didn't have to plant your Spirit in our hearts, but you do . . . .you live in us. Thank you, we love you. Help us to give you the worship you deserve; humble our hearts to trust you. Amen.

Truth, Lies, and Declaration
– Jessica Skiles –

Pause:

What comes to your mind when you think of God? A.W. Tozer once said that the answer to this question is the "most important thing about us."[18] Take a moment to think over what we've studied the last few weeks–what names and attributes of God come to mind?

Choose one of these names or attributes (light, truth, Father, etc.) to anchor your thoughts as we begin our time of prayer. Set a timer for three minutes and breathe deeply. When your thoughts begin to wander, use this word to draw you back.

Centering Prayer:

Father, thank you for being present with us. You are already here, so help me to show up and truly listen. I surrender my thoughts and attitudes to you, please shape them to look more like Christ. I am yours.

Truth, Lies, And Declaration:

Find a quiet place and open up 1 John 5. Read through verses 11-21 several times slowly – out loud if possible–asking God to guide you through this process:

Truth: *"Father, what truth do you want me to see?"* As you read, write down the truths that stand out to you. What do these verses teach us about God? What do they say about us?

Lies: *"Are there any lies that I have been believing that oppose this truth?"* Renounce these and replace them with the truth that God just showed you.

For example: *"God, I've been believing that my prayers for _____ won't actually make a difference. But you've invited me to pray, with the intention of doing something in response to those prayers. Thank you!"*

Declaration: Write down a declaration of truth and put it somewhere you'll see it often: your bathroom mirror, car, etc. Read it to yourself throughout the week and pray for God to transform your thinking in this area.

Closing Prayer:

Lord, please transform my heart and renew my mind. Let my life be a living sacrifice before you, may your truth guide my thoughts and attitudes. I am yours. Amen.

What truth do you want me to see in this chapter?

_____

_____

_____

_____

_____

_____

_____

_____

Are there any lies that I have been believing that oppose this truth?

_____

_____

_____

_____

_____

_____

_____

_____

What declaration of truth do you have for me today?

_____

_____

_____

_____

_____

_____

_____

_____

Lectio Divina
– Michelle Schaffer –

Pause:

Lord, in this time of Lectio Divina, silence my mind, my heart and my soul to hear you. Let the stillness and quiet be a time of reflection and rest as I read your word and hear your voice. Give me the ears to hear; guide me and speak to my heart today, Lord. As I take in deep breaths and long exhales, I answer the invitation to quiet myself at the feet of Jesus: inhaling his truth and exhaling any lies that hinder me from hearing his truth.

Take a couple minutes to sit in the joy of the mystery that comes with the silence, feeling the love of the Father as he guides you and speaks to you during this time of Lectio Divina.

Opening Prayer:

Lord, I know you want to speak to me today through your word and through your voice of truth. As I read the scripture you have set before me today, overwhelm me with your calmness, your clarity and your insight. I dive into this time of peace and into this time with you, Lord. Whether this time with you is full of conversation or a time of complete silence, I receive whatever you have for me today. I am ready to embrace this moment with you, Lord. I am ready to hear from you. I am ready to rest in you.

Lectio Divina:[4]

Lectio (Read): Read 1 John 5:1-5. Take a minute or two and take

---

4. Tips for Lectio Divina: Light a candle, some incense, or even an oil diffuser as a reminder of our prayer and contemplation rising up to the Father. Whenever your mind starts to wander, these can be helpful images to get you focused again.

note or highlight anything that jumps out at you. Don't feel like you need to force anything. Just allow the Spirit to intervene and guide you to what is being placed in your mind and in your heart. Allow God to guide this *Lectio*.

Mediatio (Reflect): Read 1 John 5:1-5. Take a minute or two to reflect further on the parts of scripture that stood out to you most in your last reading. Re-read these verses, or even just simple words from the passage slowly out loud and quietly in your heart. Allow God to guide you further to what he is trying to tell you in this passage. Ask him to make his voice clear and ask him to show you the truth he wants you to know.

Oratio (Respond): Read 1 John 5:1-5. Take another minute or two to respond to what God is saying to you through this reading of scripture. Feel free to pray this part aloud or even journal your response. Ask questions or write down what the Spirit puts on your heart. Maybe God wants you to know something about him, about yourself or about someone else. Maybe it's a phrase that came to mind, or a prayer or conviction in your heart. Whatever has been laid on your heart, respond and talk to the Father.

Contemplatio (Rest): Read 1 John 5:1-5 one last time. Take however long you need to rest in silent contemplation. This isn't really a time of prayer or meditation but a time to just sit in the presence of God in silence. Allow him to renew and transform you by just being in his midst. Sit still in his mystery, sit still in his embrace and allow him to work, allow him to rejuvenate your mind, body and soul. All you have to do is rest in him.

Closing Prayer:

I embrace you, Father, and I rest in you today. Thank you for your Spirit which allows me to be with you anywhere and anytime. Thank you for spending time with me and thank you for speaking with me. May I continue to meditate on your word through the day and at night, and even as I go about my day may you help me to hear your voice. As I end this Lectio Divina, may I continue to rest in you. All the glory, honor and praise be unto you. Amen.

Word or Phrase

Image

How is God inviting you to respond?

_____

_____

_____

_____

_____

_____

_____

_____

_____

_____

_____

_____

_____

_____

_____

_____

_____

_____

_____

_____

_____

_____

_____

_____

_____

_____

Obedience

– Jessica Skiles –

Pause:

"Do you trust me?" "Yes, Jesus, I trust you."

For a season, this was nearly a daily conversation between Jesus and me. When the world seemed uncertain, where my place in it seemed so small, it was this simple question that drew me back.

"Do you trust that I see your need?"

"Do you trust that I'm guiding your steps?"

"Do you trust that I love them more than you do?"

This section invites us to *ask God* to intervene. With any ask, there is always an element of trust: I *trust* that you are listening. I *trust* that you care. I *trust* that you want to bring good things into my life.

Set a timer for three minutes, breathe deeply, and lift this question before the Father. Whether you feel like you're in a great place or are really struggling to trust him, don't feel like you have to figure it out right now. Just hold it out before him.

Opening Prayer:

Father, you've invited us to pray and promised you would listen. Help me to trust you are here, that you are good, and that you are responsive.

Obedience:

Read 1 John 5:13-21 slowly. How do you see God take the initiative in shielding our faith? How might this affect the way you pray for yourself and others?

_____

_____

_____

_____

_____

When the sin of a friend, spouse, family member or church leader comes to light, we often react in a variety of ways. Our hearts sink into our stomachs and we worry; we cry. We gossip and lecture. We despair.

Read 1 John 5:14-16 one more time. Open your hands and ask God, *"Who do I need to trust you with today?"* One by one, lift these names to the Father, trusting that he loves every one of them more than you ever could.[5]

Closing Prayer:

Father, I place these people in your hands. I trust you to guide and protect them, to speak truth, to bring transformation. Please teach me how to love them in the process. Amen.

---

5. See also Luke 11:5-13.

Art
– Jessica Skiles –

Pause:

Friends . . . you have made it to the final day! Thank you for joining me on this journey of listening to God's heart – I pray that you have experienced Jesus' presence in a very real way.

For our last *Pause* exercise, I invite you to open your hands before the Lord in gratitude, worship, and surrender. Breathe deeply and invite the Holy Spirit to draw your attention to the truths he has shown you these past few weeks.

Opening Prayer:

Father, thank you for giving us your Word – offering us light, guidance, and hope. Your presence transforms us, so thank you for choosing to come, to speak, to live in us. We are listening; open our hearts to receive you.

Art:

Over the past few weeks, we've engaged with several art forms: poetry, photography, creative writing, painting. These creative elements help us break out of our prayer "boxes" : to invite Jesus into our creativity and to see him in the places we maybe weren't looking for him before. They help us to slow down and *delight* in God, rather than check him off the to-do list.

So today as you read, I'm going to invite you to create your *own* art response: to worship and spend time with God slowly in whatever way that he may have wired you. Try something you love or try something new.[6] As you read through 1 John 5:18-21, some ideas of how to engage it creatively include:

- **PAINT:** What images come to mind as you read this passage? Paint or sketch what you see.

- **WORD ART:** Read this passage slowly, doodling any words or attributes of God that stand out to you.

- **MUSIC:** Choose a few phrases or truths about God from this section. Put these verbatim to a tune or use them as building blocks for writing your own song!

- **OTHER IDEAS:** Snap a photo, write a poem, mold some clay, take a nature walk, embroider a pillow. Ask God to open your eyes to see him in these everyday things you enjoy and allow yourself to *be* with him in that experience. Let his Word shape the art you create.

Closing Prayer:

Father, thank you for being a God of life, of truth, of freedom. You have loved us so much more fully than we can really understand, but help us to press more deeply into it every day. We love you . . . help us to love one another. Amen.

---

6. If you're a perfectionist or consider yourself "not artsy" – remember that no one has to see this! This is an opportunity to remember that God created every part of us – our intellect, emotions, voice, body – they all can reflect his glory and point us back to him.

ENDNOTES

1. All Scripture quotations will be from the 2011 NIV unless otherwise noted.

2. Some say that it was written by a disciple of John the Apostle. Ian Howard Marshall, *The Epistles of John*, (Grand Rapids, MI: Eerdmans, 2009), 40-46 SilvaMoisés and Merrill C Tenney, *The Zondervan Encyclopedia of the Bible: Volume 3* (Grand Rapids, MI: Zondervan, 2009), 729

3. D. Nässelqvist, *John the Apostle. The Lexham Bible Dictionary*. (Bellingham, WA: Lexham Press, 2016)

4. Guzik, David. "1 John 2:1-6 – The One Who Makes Relationship Possible". *The Book of 1 John*. Enduring Word Commentary Series, October 21, 2017

5. SilvaMoisés, *The Zondervan Encyclopedia of the Bible: Volume 3*, 729, 760-761

6. Robert W.m Yarbrough, *1-3 John*, (Grand Rapids, MI: Baker Academic, 2008), 17

7. Michael Gagarin, *The Oxford Encyclopedia of Ancient Greek and Rome: Volume 1*. (Oxford, UK: Oxford University Press, 2010), lxxix-lxxx; Michael Gagarin, *The Oxford Encyclopedia of Ancient Greek and Rome: Volume 3*. (Oxford, UK: Oxford University Press, 2010), 78-81

8. Marshall, *The Epistles of John*, 14-15; SilvaMoisés, *The Zondervan Encyclopedia of the Bible: Volume 3*, 725-726

9. Marshall, *The Epistles of John*, 54-55

10. Shiflett, Diana. *Spiritual Practices in Community: Drawing Groups into the Heart of God*. (Downers Grove, IL: IVP Books, An Imprint of Intervarsity Press, 2018), 30-31

11. SilvaMoisés, *The Zondervan Encyclopedia of the Bible: Volume 3*, 727-732

12. David G. Benner, *Opening to God: Lectio Divina and Life as Prayer* (Downers Grove, IL: InterVarsity Press, 2010), 48

13. Encyclopedia of the Bible, Volume 3, 734; Vincent, M. R. (1887). Word studies in the New Testament (Vol. 1, pp. 456–457). New York, NY: Charles Scribner's Sons.

14. John 13:35

15. Elizabeth Elliot, "MARRIAGE: A REVOLUTION and a REVELATION a Supreme Earthly Test of Discipleship." Accessed December 31, 2021. https://womenlivingwell.org/wp-content/uploads/2014/07/Elisabeth-Elliot-Marriage-draft.pdf.

16. Gerhard Kittel, *Theological Dictionary of the New Testament: Volume 1*. (Grand Rapids, Mich. Eerdmans, 2006), 22-45; Marshall, *The Epistles of John*, 205-211; B.I. Simpson, "Love." In J.D. Barr, D. Bomar, D.R. Brown, R. Klippenstein, D. Mangum, C. Sinclair Wolcott, . . . W. Widder (Eds.), The Lexham Bible Dictionary. (Bellingham, WA: Lexham Press, 2016)

17. Marshall, *The Epistles of John*, 230-235; Gary M. Burge, *The NIV Application Commentary: Letters of John*. (Grand Rapids, MI: Zondervan, 1996), 200-204

18. Tozer, A.W., *The Knowledge of the Holy* (New York, NY: HarperCollins, 1978), 1.

RESOURCES

Books

- *Spiritual Practices in Community* by Diana Shifflett

- *Women of the Word: How to Study the Bible with Both Our Hearts and Our Minds* by Jen Wilkin

- *Opening to God: Learning Lectio Divina and Life as Prayer* by David G. Benner

- *Praying in Color: Drawing a New Path to God* by Sybil MacBeth

Apps

- Pause

- Lectio365

Podcasts

- "Strengthening the Soul of Your Leadership" by Ruth Haley Barton

Videos

- "Next Level Series: Prayer" by Michael Defazio

REFERENCES

Alexander, David, and Pat Alexander. *Zondervan Handbook to the Bible.* Grand Rapids, MI: Zondervan Pub. House, 2017

Burge, Gary M. *The NIV Application Commentary: Letters of John.* Grand Rapids, MI: Zondervan Pub. House, 1996

Collegeville Institute, and Laura Kelly Fanucci. "The Practice of Group Lectio Divina," 2016. Accessed July 6, 2021. *https://www.communitiesofcalling.org/wp-content/uploads/2018/09/Lectio-Divina-Guide.pdf.*

Elliot, Elisabeth. n.d. "MARRIAGE: A REVOLUTION and a REVELATION a Supreme Earthly Test of Discipleship." Accessed December 31, 2021. *https://womenlivingwell.org/wp-content/uploads/2014/07/Elisabeth-Elliot-Marriage-draft.pdf.*

"Engaging the Scriptures for Transformation." Directed by Ruth Haley Barton. Produced by Transforming Center. April 12, 2017. Podcast, 0:34. *https://transformingcenter.org/2017/04/episode-4-engaging-scriptures-transformation/*

Gagarin, Michael. *The Oxford Encyclopedia of Ancient Greek and Rome: Volume 3.* Oxford: UK, Oxford University Press, 2010

Gagarin, Michael. *The Oxford Encyclopedia of Ancient Greek and Rome: Volume 1.* Oxford: UK, Oxford University Press, 2010

Keener, Craig S, and Intervarsity Press. *The IVP Bible Background Commentary: New Testament.* Downers Grove, IL: Intervarsity Press, 2014

Kittel, Gerhard, Geoffrey William, and Gerhard Friedrich. *Theological Dictionary of the New Testament.* Grand Rapids, MI: Eerdmans, 2006

MacArthur, John. *The MacArthur New Testament Commentary: 1-3 John.* Chicago, IL: Moody Publishers, 2007

Marshall, Howard. 1978. *The New International Commentary on the New Testament: The Epistles of John.* Grand Rapids, MI: Eerdmans, 2009

Nässelqvist, D. "John the Apostle." In J. D. Barry, D. Bomar, D. R. Brown, R. Klippenstein, D.

Mangum, C. Sinclair Wolcott, . . . W. Widder (Eds.), *The Lexham Bible Dictionary*. Bellingham, WA: Lexham Press, 2016

"Overview: 1-3 John." Produced by Bible Project. December 11, 2016. YouTube video, 9:35. *https://www.youtube.com/watch?v=l3QkE6nKylM*

"Prayer – Deepening Our Intimacy with God." Directed by Ruth Haley Barton. Produced by Transforming Center. April 5, 2017. Podcast, 0:40. *https:// transformingcenter.org/2017/04/episode-3-prayer-deepening-intimacy-god/*

Shiflett, Diana. *Spiritual Practices in Community: Drawing Groups into the Heart of God*. Downers Grove, IL: IVP Books, An Imprint of Intervarsity Press, 2018

SilvaMoisés, and Merrill C Tenney. *The Zondervan Encyclopedia of the Bible: Volume 3, H-L*. Grand Rapids, MI: Zondervan, 2009

Simpson, B. I. "Love" in J. D. Barry, D. Bomar, D. R. Brown, R. Klippenstein, D. Mangum, C. Sinclair Wolcott, . . . W. Widder (Eds.), *The Lexham Bible Dictionary*. Bellingham, WA: Lexham Press, 2016

"The Book of 1 John." Directed by David Guzik. Produced by Enduring Word Commentary Series Podcast. Oct. 19-Nov. 5, 2017. Apple Podcast. *https:// podcasts.apple.com/us/podcast/the-book-of-1-john-enduring-word-media-server/ id1411841306*

Tozer, A.W. *The Knowledge of the Holy*. New York, NY: HarperCollins, 1978

Vincent, M. R. *Word Studies in the New Testament*, Vol. 1. New York, NY: Charles Scribner's Sons, 1887

Vincent, M. R *Word Studies in the New Testament*, Vol. 2. New York, NY: Charles Scribner's Sons, 1887

Wilkin, Jen. *Women of the Word: How to Study the Bible with Both Our Hearts and Our Minds*. Wheaton: Crossway, 2019

Yarbrough, Robert W. *1-3 John*. Grand Rapids, MI: Baker Academic, 2008

www.ingramcontent.com/pod-product-compliance
Lightning Source LLC
LaVergne TN
LVHW010307070426
835511LV00027B/3496